KEYBOARD
GUIDE

Jeromy Bessler and Norbert Opgenoorth

VOGGENREITER PUBLISHERS
P. O. Box 210126, 53156 Bonn/Germany
www.voggenreiter.de
info@voggenreiter.de
Typesetting and Layout: B & O

Contents

I. PREFACE

This "Keyboard Guide" shows the chords and their voicings, scales and harmonic relationships - in short: some of the material comprising the building blocks of Western music - in compact form. This small guide is not intended to replace a piano course, a qualified teacher or thorough studies of harmony and theory. It is intended to be used as a reference in daily practice.
Those of you who are interested in a more thorough study of these subjects will find some remarks on scales, their construction and music theory in the second chapter. Additionally, there is a section on chords, inversions and voicings.

The third chapter contains diagrams in all twelve keys with eight pages per key, of which:

1. The first three sides of each key are beginner to intermediate level. Here, the most basic scales, easy inversions, intervals (relations to the root note) and related keys are shown. Most of the diagrams are given with fingerings, to facilitate using them in a practical musical situation.
2. The next five pages show the most common chords and scales. This material was written with the intermediate or even advanced player in mind. It can be useful in composing, rehearsing or improvising.

Some suggestions on using your "Keyboard Guide":

Enharmonically interchangeable chords (for example G♯ and A♭) are only notated in the version with a flat (with the exception of the key of F♯/G♭).
We chose this form, in order to keep the number of accidentals, to a minimum, and to make the chords as easy to read as possible.

If chords are viewed in a (harmonic) context or in relation to each other, they have to be notated accordingly: e.g., the dominant (V) chord in the key of G♯ is D♯, not E♭ !

Chord Diagrams in all Keys

The first page of every key starts with an illustration of the **major scale**, shown here in the key of C. These scales are depicted in standard notation as well as in a diagram of the keys on the piano.
The structure of a given scale (the location of the half and whole steps) is given in the standard notation.
Use the fingering pattern given in the diagram:

Fingering   1 2 3 1 2 3 4 5

whole step   half step

The three **minor scales** come next: For the augmented second (three half steps) contained only in the harmonic minor scale, the following sign is used: ⌣ .

The second page of each key contains the **inversions** of the major and minor triads and their nearest harmonic relationships:
the dominant (V), subdominant (IV) and the parallel minor chord (VI) of the tonic.

All the chords are given with fingerings:

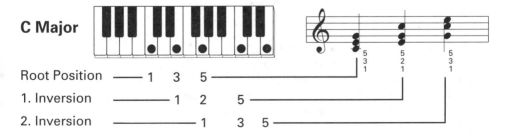

C Major

Root Position ——— 1   3   5 —————————

1. Inversion   ———— 1   2   5 —————————

2. Inversion   ————— 1   3   5 —————————

The third page of each key contains some basic theory: **intervals** and the **circle of fifths**. These subjects may not be very useful for the beginner, but will prove their importance later on in your musical development.

We start with a look at the most common **intervals,** shown from the root of the corresponding key. These are not all the possible intervals in the given key, just some of the most widely used.

1	♭2	2	♭3	3	4	#4	♭5	5	#5	♭6	6	7	maj7	8	♭9	9	10	11
Unison	Minor Second	Major Second	Minor Third	Major Third	Fourth	Augmented Fourth	Diminished Fifth	Fifth	Augmented Fifth	Minor Sixth	Major Sixth	Minor Seventh	Major Seventh	Octave	Minor Ninth	Major Ninth	Tenth	Eleventh

The **circle of fifths** is a powerful tool for demonstrating and analyzing musical relationships between chords and keys. Since this is not a music theory workbook, the following explanations are kept to the absolute minimum. Lots of good theory books are available on the subject.

The circle of fifths is built by stacking perfect fifths simultaneously upward and downward from a given root (here: C). Because notes can be enharmonically changed in tempered tuning, those stacks of fifths meet a tritone apart from the root (here: F#/G♭). Harmonies and keys in the circle of fifths are notated using using sharps in the right half of the circle, flats in the left half. The most basic rule for using the circle is: the farther apart two harmonies or keys in the circle of fifths, the less harmonically related they are. The most important chords in any key are the ones next to each other in the circle of

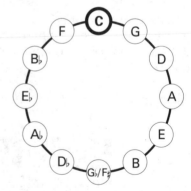

fifths: tonic, subdominant and dominant chord. In the example above: C major, F major and G major. Another chord used frequently is the double dominant chord (the dominant chord of the dominant chord, here: D major.

The illustrations only show a portion of the circle of fifths in any given key. This was done to keep things as simple as possible and because the other harmonic relationships aren't used as often.

If you want to complete the circle of fifths of a given key, you should be able to do this yourself (hint: building the circle yourself from all the roots and checking the results will tremendously train your ability to recognize the relationships between two or more chords in a song or chord progression). However, we added the most important "third relations" to the circle of fifths:

- **relative minor chord** (the triad built on the sixth step of the major scale) is most closely related to the tonic chord.
  The scales of the tonic (C major) and the relative minor chord (A minor) contain exactly the same notes and use the same accidentals.

- **mediants** and **submediants**: we use this term for the relationship between any two chords a third apart. Using C major as the tonal center for our example, these would be A♭ major and E major.
  Mediants and submediants are often called "major third relations".

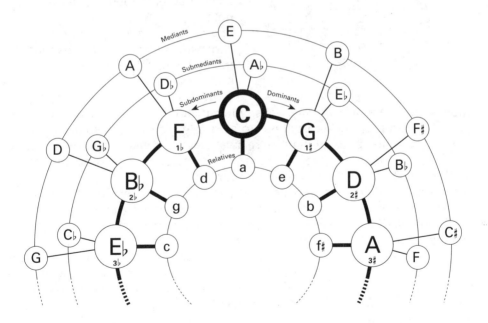

II. SOME THEORY

Chords

Basically, any number of notes played simultaneously can be regarded as a chord. However, there are many rules concerning the actual note choice for a given chord. You should know at least some of these rules to improve your understanding and use of chords in your playing.

In traditional Western harmony, chords always consist of stacked thirds. Depending on the type of chord desired, major and minor thirds can be combined in many different ways. Starting with the basic major triad, this stacking of thirds can be continued right up to the 7/9/11/13 chord (this chord can be thought of as all the notes of a major scale played simultaneously).

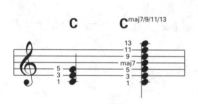

The number "15" is given to the root, transposed up an octave. Added notes not contained in the basic triad are thought of as "tension notes'.

The numerals given to the notes of a chord derive from the corresponding major scale, for example "3" means major third; "♭3" minor third, and so forth.

Chords can be varied in many ways: you can add notes to an existing chord (e.g., the sixth), replace chord tones (e.g., use the fourth instead of the third), alter chord tones by flattening or raising them and many combinations of the ones mentioned above. There is, however, one small problem: which combinations of chord tones sound good?

There are lots of rules on chord construction, many of them are useful, some completely useless. Music is (and should be) a constantly evolving art-form. Therefore, all of its rules are evolving, too. For instance, many of todays harmonies would have been unthinkable in the 16th century.

A thorough study of harmony and music theory in general is one of the most important ways to achieve a better understanding of what you are doing and to expand your creativity, but you should also always be aware that music only evolves by trying out new ideas. In our humble opinion, it all boils down to the simple idea of knowing the rules before bending (or breaking) them.

Today's music has been heavily influenced by harmonic concepts used in Blues and - especially - Jazz. Compared to "Classical" harmony, Jazz harmony differs in the understanding and use of consonant and dissonant chords. Jazz harmony may well be the single most important development in 20th century music theory. A thorough study of Jazz harmony and melody is one of the best methods of broadening your musical horizon and general understanding of music.

You can build quite a lot of chords from the twelve notes of the chromatic scale. Depending on your personal tastes and hearing experiences, some of them may not be very pleasant.

There is, however, a kind of "common ground", a repertoire of chords heavily used in all kinds of music, even if most Rock/Pop-songs only use a small percentage of them. We have tried to present these chords in an easy-to-use and systematic format.

They are therefore grouped together in "chord families": major, minor and seventh, and - last not least - diminished and augmented chords.

This grouping of chords into families has proven to be of great practical use, and makes it easier to find chords quickly and conveniently.

The first page of each key is dedicated to **major chords**:
- the easy basic chords with an added sixth or ninth
- the sus2 and sus4 chord, the third is substituted by the second or fourth
- chords with a major seventh (maj7)

Again, this is just a selection from the vast number of chords theoretically possible.

Another page contains the **minor chords**:

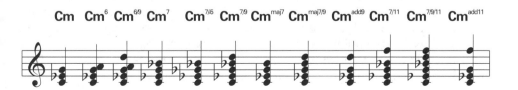

Seventh chords are by far the group of chords with the most members. They all contain the minor (or dominant) seventh. In traditional harmony, these chords are thought of as tension chords, meaning they have to be resolved into their corresponding tonic chord (down a fifth). Today, the dominant function of these chords still remains important, although modern composers don't consider it absolutely necessary (especially in Jazz- and Blues-related forms of music) to resolve these chords to their tonic chords.

The **diminished** and the **augmented** chord don't really belong to any of the "chord families" mentioned above, and are therefore notated separately here.

While the diminished chord consists of two minor thirds, the augmented chord consists of two major thirds.

In some playing situations, another minor third is added to the diminished chord, making it a so-called **diminished seventh chord**.

In all charts, the diminished chord is notated as a diminished seventh chord.

Suggestion: there are really just three diminished and four augmented chords: you can build a diminished chord from the roots C, C♯/D♭ and D; the diminished chord with the root E♭ contains the same notes (enharmonically changed) as the diminished chord with the root C. Using the same principle with the augmented chord, you can build four augmented chords; the fifth chord again consists of the same notes (enharmonically changed) as the first.

Some chord symbols may look a little complicated at first, so here are a few guidelines for deciphering them:

- the seventh (7) is always given first in the chord symbol.
  It is regarded as part of the chord, not as an option (as, for example, are the ninth, eleventh and thirteenth).
- whenever a chord contains a seventh (7) and a sixth (6), the sixth is called a thirteenth (13). This is done to clearly show the structure of the chord.
- "add"-options are added to the basic chord, "sus"-extensions replace the third of the basic chord.
- if a chord contains a ♭5 (flatted fifth) or a ♯5 (raised fifth), these altered chord tones replace the fifth of the basic chord. Again, to show the tertiary structure of the chord, these are indicated as ♯11 or ♭13, but are also given transposed down an octave in parentheses: ♯11 (♭5) and ♭13 (♯5).
  This isn't really correct, neither notation-wise nor theoretically. We have used this simplification on purpose because, in the tempered tuning system the ♭5 and the ♯11 (or ♯5 and ♭13) are the same pitches and, in real-life situations you often find both interval names used interchangeably.

Inversions and Voicings

A given chord can have many different forms. These forms are often called voicings. The most basic voicing is the "root position': all chord tones are stacked in thirds on top of each other. Another way of arranging the notes of a given chord is to build so-called **inversions**. This simply means transposing the lowest voice of a chord up an octave, making it the melody note. Using a triad, you can build two inversions:

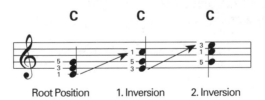

Root Position   1. Inversion   2. Inversion

Yet another way of voicing a chord is the "wide position'. A chord is said to be in a wide position if you can insert another one of its chord tones between any two of its tones:

Naturally, you can also invert chords in wide position.

Wide Position

Sounds good so far? There is, however, one little problem: many chords don't sound so good in their "normal" inverted form. For the example below we took a $C^{maj7\flat9}$ chord and simply built the first inversion. Most people will probably agree, that this chord sounds quite awful. There are three chord tones voiced a half step apart from each other:

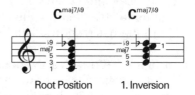

Root Position   1. Inversion

As you can see, simply inverting this chord just isn't enough to get a satisfying sound; you have to think about **chord voicings**. We use the term **voicing** for all the different techniques to arrange the chord tones of a given chord. There are countless voicing techniques, of which here are just two examples:

- **drop 2**: in Jazz, this is a quite common voicing technique.
  To get a drop 2 voicing, simply transpose the second voice of the chord down an octave.

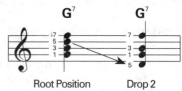

Root Position   Drop 2

- **drop 3** and **drop 2+4**: these drop variants are not very common. However, the principle remains the same: the indicated voices are transposed down an octave.

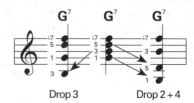

Drop 3   Drop 2 + 4

- You can also "invert" the drop-techniques, transposing chord tones up an octave.

- Another way of voicing chords is to leave out some of the chord tones. Be careful to keep the chord recognizable, though.

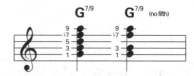

  You should always have an open ear for your fellow musicians. As a rule of thumb, you can omit the chord tones already being played by other musicians in your own voicings. For instance, playing with a bass player, the root (normally the singlemost important chord tone) can often be omitted, since the bass player will be playing it already.

One thing to remember: you should always avoid voicing tension notes in the bass range. These can become much too dissonant and overpowering, dominate the whole chord and thus endanger its function.

It should be mentioned again that all of these rules are just rough guidelines among many others. The advantages of a serious study of musical theory can't be stressed enough!

Another thing you should be aware of is to never view a chord in isolation, but always connected to its musical background, because this can heavily influence the appropriate voicing. The melody of a song, its harmonies, chord progressions and your own personal taste are all parameters that can't really be restricted by rules.

And yet another suggestion: music always comes first, rules follow second!

A serious composer - regardless of musical styles, trends or the age he lives in - shouldn't be restricted by rules. In fact, he has to break them sometimes! There will always be (and always have been) people who like to see music as a strict network of never-changing rules; really great music has always been composed by the other ones.

The chord charts in this book are sorted according to the chord options and alterations. This means a "7/13 chord" follows after a "7/9 chord'. Each chord has its own stylized piano key chart. This illustration shows the chord in its root position. It is also the first voicing notated on the musical staff to the right of each chord graphic. To put it in another way: all the chord tones are notated stacked in thirds on top of each other:

C_m^{add9}

Additionally, there are three voicings notated as examples. These aren't the only ones possible, just some voicings we prefer. Those are sometimes drop-variants, sometimes wide positions, sometimes just simple inversions. The voicings are just suggestions or starting points; they have to be adapted to a particular musical surrounding. In fact, this is where the fun starts. Try them yourself ...

A topic we can't discuss here is the division of chord tones between your hands (you could write a whole book on this subject alone). Some of the chords sound good if you play the two lowest voices with the left hand, others using drop technique, still others have a nice tone if you play root and seventh with the left and all other chord tones with the right hand.

We think the best way is to experiment for yourself. This is the reason why all the chords are notated in treble clef only.

Scales

This chapter concentrates on the most important scales used in composing and improvising. These scales are just a small selection from the vast number of scales theoretically possible.

The first part of this chapter consists of explanations regarding the scales notated in every key, the second part (special scales) contains scales that aren't notated in each key but must be transposed, if needed. Each scale is given with its interval structure (as always, compared to the major scale). This is meant to make understanding a particular scale and its use easy and can also be a tremendous help in analyzing and comparing different scales. Most of these scales can bear a lot of different names, depending on their source, so the interval structure can also help to clear the smoke here.

Most of the scales are given with some - selected - possibilities of using them. These are only suggestions, no unbreakable rules. You should experiment using these scales wherever you like, according to your own personal taste.

As with the other chapters, this part of the "Keyboard Guide" is by no means intended to replace more specialized books on the subjects of harmony and improvisation, but to give you a general idea of the concepts and ideas, and to provide some kind of starting ground on which to base your further studies.

Major Scale and its Modes

The major scale builds the basis of Western harmony; it is the rule used in measuring all other scales. The most basic major scale is the C major scale (no accidentals). It is shown below with its interval structure. Arabic numerals are used to indicate the intervals contained in the major scale (for example "3" always means major third). This way, the interval structure of every scale can be compared to that of the major scale. Scale tones differing from the major scale, with the same root, are indicated with ♯ and ♭ (for example, a minor third would be called ♭3).

1 2 3 4 5 6 7 8

The interval structure can be seen as a "blueprint" for all the major scales, indicating all their intervals and their order.

Following this blueprint, you can build a major scale from each of the twelve tones of the tempered system. You simply change the starting tone (the root), but keep the interval structure.

The following diagram shows this, using the D major scale as an example:

1 2 3 4 5 6 7 8

Remember: the actual notes change, the interval structure remains the same.

You can also invert the above-mentioned principle "the notes change, the interval structure remains the same" to "the notes remain constant, the interval structure changes". Sounds a bit fuzzy? Here's how it works:

Play the notes of a C major scale, first from C to C, then from D to D; from E to E and so on, until you reach C one octave higher than your starting point. You'll get seven different scales, each one containing the notes of C major, each one with its very own interval structure and sound. These seven scales are called the modes of C major. They form a "family" (sometimes called modal system) of scales.

While our major/minor system is still very young, these modes are a lot older. They are named after various greek tribes. We notated them below, starting from the root C. To better show their differences and similarities, their interval structure is indicated, too.

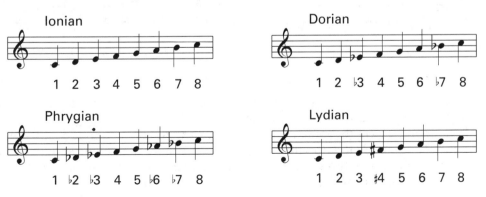

Ionian

1 2 3 4 5 6 7 8

Dorian

1 2 ♭3 4 5 6 ♭7 8

Phrygian

1 ♭2 ♭3 4 5 ♭6 ♭7 8

Lydian

1 2 3 ♯4 5 6 7 8

Mixolydian

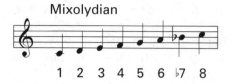

1 2 3 4 5 6 ♭7 8

Aeolian

1 2 ♭3 4 5 ♭6 ♭7 8

Locrian

1 ♭2 ♭3 4 ♭5 ♭6 ♭7 8

Note: we took a little liberty in deriving the modes from the major scale. This isn't really correct, since the modes are by far the older system. As a matter of fact, it's exactly the other way around: the major scale is the first of the modes, the (natural) minor scale the sixth. These simply were the most popular of the modes. Modes and the minor/major system aren't really two different systems, but two different ways of looking at the same (musical) facts.

On the previous page we showed you how to build a major scale from any given note applying the interval structure (or "blueprint") to a different root. You can build the modes from every root in exactly the same way: applying the interval structure to a different root, the actual notes change, but the interval structure remains constant.
Below is an example showing this with the dorian mode. We notated it first with the root D, then with the root E:

1 2 ♭3 4 5 6 ♭7 8

1 2 ♭3 4 5 6 ♭7 8

By looking at the interval symbols of the modes, you can see that some of them are major-, some minor-sounding.
Major-sounding are the ionian (major), lydian and mixolydian mode.
Minor-sounding are the dorian, phrygian and aeolian mode (natural minor).
The locrian mode is the exception, being neither major- nor minor-related, but most closely related to the diminished seventh chord.

Each of the modes can be used to improvise over its corresponding chord.
This principle is shown in the diagram to the right, in the key of C major.

1st Step	Ionian	$C^{maj7\ (9/11/13)}$
2nd Step	Dorian	$Dm^{7\ (9/11/13)}$
3rd Step	Phrygian	$Em^{7\ (\flat9/11/\flat13)}$
4th Step	Lydian	$Fmaj7\ (9/\sharp11/13)$
5th Step	Mixolydian	$G^{7\ (9/11/13)}$
6th Step	Aeolian	$Am^{7\ (9/11/b13)}$
7th Step	Locrian	$Bm^{7/\flat5\ (\flat9/11/\flat13)}$

Natural Minor Scale

Each major scale has a so-called "relative" minor scale (with its root a minor third lower), using the same notes and the same accidentals. This scale is called **natural minor scale**. It is identical to (derived from) the 5th mode of its relative major scale.
In other words: the 5th mode of the C major scale (aeolian) is the "relative" minor scale: A minor. The same principle applies to all the other major scales.
Starting from a different root, the interval structure of the natural minor scale is very different from that of the relative major scale, even if both use identical notes.

1　2　♭3　4　5　♭6　♭7　8

You could build a modal system from the natural minor scale. This does not really make much sense, because the natural minor scale contains exactly the same notes as its relative major scale - and therefore the same modes ...

Harmonic Minor Scale and its Modes

The chord built from the fifth step of the natural minor scale (the dominant chord) is a minor chord. Because a major dominant chord sounds very good in the "classical cadenza" (the third of the major dominant chord can be very nicely resolved to the root of the tonic chord), a major dominant chord is quite often used in minor keys.
To obtain a major dominant chord in a minor key, you have to raise the seventh scale step.
The resulting scale is called the **harmonic minor scale**:

1　2　♭3　4　5　♭6　7　8

Since the harmonic minor is a seven-note scale, you can build seven modes from it. This is done exactly the same way as with the major scale on the previous page. There are lots of different names used for the modes of the harmonic minor scale, so we gave them numbers: HM 1, HM 2, HM 3 and so forth. These seven modes are listed below (in the key of C minor), together with the most common names used for them:

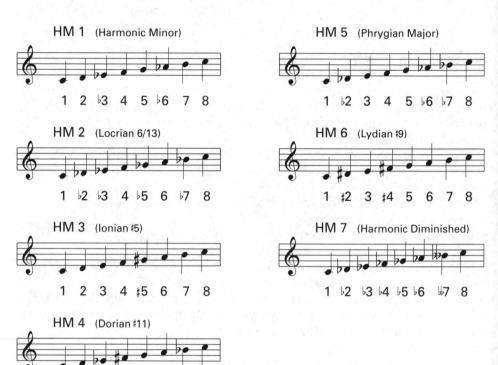

HM 1 (Harmonic Minor)
1 2 ♭3 4 5 ♭6 7 8

HM 2 (Locrian 6/13)
1 ♭2 ♭3 4 ♭5 6 ♭7 8

HM 3 (Ionian ♯5)
1 2 3 4 ♯5 6 7 8

HM 4 (Dorian ♯11)
1 2 ♭3 ♯4 5 6 ♭7 8

HM 5 (Phrygian Major)
1 ♭2 3 4 5 ♭6 ♭7 8

HM 6 (Lydian ♯9)
1 ♯2 3 ♯4 5 6 7 8

HM 7 (Harmonic Diminished)
1 ♭2 ♭3 ♭4 ♭5 ♭6 ♭♭7 8

In the chapter on scales of each key, only the most commonly used modes of the harmonic minor scale are notated to keep the number of scales manageable. These are:

1. Harmonic minor, 3rd mode: this scale can be used to improvise over a M7/♭5-chord.
2. Harmonic minor, 5th mode: can be played over a V chord (major dominant chord) in a minor key.

Melodic Minor Scale and its Modes

The harmonic minor scale contains the interval of an augmented second (from the sixth to the seventh scale step). To get a diatonic scale (meaning: a scale consisting only of minor and major seconds), the sixth note in the scale has to be raised as well. The resulting scale (a natural minor scale with a ♯6 and ♯7 or a major scale with a ♭3, depending on the point of view) is called **melodic minor scale**. In "Classical" harmony, there are two forms of this scale: one ascending, and one descending:

The descending form of the melodic minor scale is identical to the natural minor scale. There is a simple rule of thumb for this scale: when ascending, play a melodic minor scale, when descending, play a natural minor scale. In Jazz, this scale is played with a ♯6 and ♯7 (compared to natural minor), no matter whether ascending or descending. The melodic minor scale can also be used to construct a modal system of scales as shown below (Root: C).

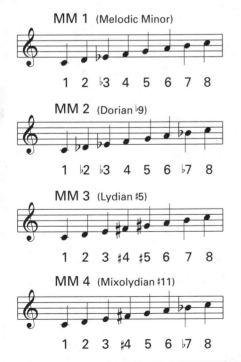

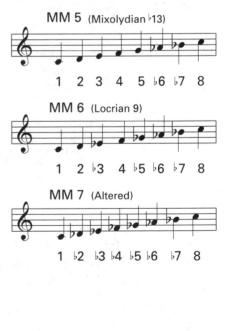

In improvisations, mostly the 1st and the 7th modes (this mode is someti-mes called the superlocrian scale) of the melodic minor scale are used. By enharmonically changing the notes of the 7th mode of the melodic minor scale, you can build the so-called altered scale. The scale is named after the fact that it contains the basic chord tones (1, 3 and ♭7) of the seventh chord, as well as the alterations (meaning in this context: lowered or raised) of ninths and fifths (♭9, ♯9, ♭5, ♯5).

The altered scale is most often used over chords from the dominant family containing altered fifths and/or ninths.

MM 7

1 ♭2 ♭3 ♭4 ♭5 ♭6 ♭7 8

Altered

1 ♭2 ♯2 3 ♭5 ♯5 ♭7 8
(♭9) (♯9)

Gypsy Minor Scale

Another member of the minor scale family is the so-called gypsy minor scale. It is easily constructed by raising the 4th scale step of the harmonic minor scale by one half step:

1 2 ♭3 ♯4 5 ♭6 ♭7 8

This is the most "oriental"-sounding scale of the minor scale family. It con-tains four(!) halfsteps and two(!) augmented seconds. This scale is mostly used melodically. You could build a modal system based on this scale, or even harmonize it with itself. We consider the results somewhat bizarre, but who are we to judge?

This scale is rarely used in improvising, but you could be just the right per-son to change this.

Major Pentatonic

Just like its "sister-scale" (the minor pentatonic), the major pentatonic scale is one of the oldest known scales. To this day, it is used in traditional music of many different cultures. Both scales are five-note scales (Greek: penta = five) and contain no half steps. The harmonic potential of this scales is not exactly overwhelming, as you can see for yourself by harmonizing them, but in the bargain you are rewarded with fantastic melodic possibilities. You can build the major pentatonic by stacking fifths on top of each other: c-g-d-a-e. Transposed into the same octave, you get the following scale:

These scales contain no halfsteps and therefore lack the leading-tone tension typical for most of Western melody and harmony. For the unexperienced listener, the pentatonic scales tend to have a somewhat "Eastern" sound. There is a special kind of attraction in the simple, beautiful structure of these scales. These scales are more ambiguous in their functionality than the other scales and certainly belong to the most loved and frequently used scales in modern music. There simply isn't any musician who doesn't use them.

Being a five-note scale, you can build five modes from the major pentatonic scale. In improvising, the fifth of these modes is the most commonly used. This fifth mode has the same relationship to its "parent scale" as the natural minor scale to the major scale: its root is a minor third below and it contains the same notes.
We have notated all the modes of the major pentatonic below:

Major Pentatonic 1

Major Pentatonic 2

Major Pentatonic 3

1 ♭3 4 ♭6 ♭7

Major Pentatonic 4

1 2 4 5 6

Major Pentatonic 5

1 ♭3 4 5 ♭7

This may well be the most "universal" of all scales. The possibilities of this scale are really endless. The most obvious one is improvising over a major chord with the same root. There are many other musical situations in which you can use this scale.

To point them all out would mean writing another book; besides, this is not the "pentatonic guide". Try analyzing this scale, with different roots over all the chords you know and ... experiment!

Minor Pentatonic

This fifth mode of the major pentatonic contains a minor third. It is most often used in improvising over minor chords in a Rock/Blues context, but there are also lots of other possibilities:

1 ♭3 4 5 ♭7 8

Suggestion: As well as thinking of the minor pentatonic as the fifth mode of the major pentatonic, you can think of the major pentatonic as the second mode of the minor pentatonic. Whichever works for you is just fine ...

Extended Minor Pentatonic

This scale is often called minor pentatonic (added ♭5). It's exactly what it says - a minor pentatonic with an added ♭5.
There are just as many places you can use this scale as with the other pentatonic scales (we'll leave this up to you).

1 ♭3 4 ♭5 5 ♭7 8

Blues Scale

This seven-note scale can be constructed by adding a major third to the extended minor pentatonic scale:

1 ♭3 3 ♭5 5 ♭7 8

Altered Pentatonic

This is a whole family of scales often used in contemporary Jazz. The basic idea is this: using a "normal" pentatonic scale as a starting point, alter (i.e., raise or lower) one of its notes to get a new scale. There are virtually endless possibilities behind this idea, so we won't even try to discuss them all. Use this concept to construct your own altered pentatonic scales and have some fun.
These kinds of scales are mostly played over dominant chords.

Major Scale with Blue Notes

The so-called "blue notes" are the attempt of Western musicians to make the characteristic intervals of Afro-American traditional music available in our system of well-tempered tuning. The blue notes got their name from their usage in the (sung) Blues of the American slaves at the beginning of the century. Those pitches that can't really be played on tempered-tuned instruments (for example: the piano) are:

- first blue note, pitched between minor and major third (substituting both),
- second blue note, a little below our perfect fifth,
- third blue note, roughly equivalent to the minor seventh.

In well-tempered tuning, the nearest approximation to the "real thing" is achieved by adding the minor third, the flatted fifth and the minor seventh to the major scale.
You can emulate the blue notes very well on instruments permitting seamless pitchbending, such as the guitar (string bending), most other stringed instruments and most wind instruments.
Many keyboarders "cheat" by playing both of the thirds or fifths simultaneously, or in short succession, or utilizing pitchbending.
To develop this "feeling" we recommend listening to as many authentic Blues recordings as you can get your sweaty hands on.

To keep things simple, we notated the major scale with blue notes just like a "normal" major scale. The blue notes are indicated with arrows pointing downward.
Their real pitch is a little below the corresponding notes in tempered tuning.

1   2   ↓3   4   ↓5   6   ↓7   8

Special Scales:

1. Chromatic Scale

The chromatic scale (Greek: chroma = color) contains all twelve notes of the Western system of tempered tuning. There is only one chromatic scale. If you like, you can derive every imaginable chord from the chromatic scale.

There are two main reasons for mentioning this scale here:
- The chromatic scale can be regarded as the "mother of all scales", with every other scale being derived from it. This point of view isn't historically correct, but can be used to great advantage in analyzing and understanding certain concepts of improvisation. The improvisations of some musicians have a very strong chromatic content.

- The chromatic scale is sometimes used (as a whole scale or in part) in composed or improvised music; there are some wonderful sounds derived from this scale.

2. Whole-Tone Scale

As the name suggests, the whole tone scale only contains whole steps. This is the most symmetrical scale, each of its notes can be thought of as the root. If you want a sample of its sound, listen to the works of the French composer Claude Debussy, who favored its use.
Moreover, there are only two different whole-tone scales.
Although it contains the three most important chord tones of the seventh chord (1, 3, ♭7), this scale hasn't the necessary structure to construct a whole tonal system from it alone. This scale is normally used to improvise over chords from the dominant family. You can play this scale over a Dom.$^{7/♭5\ (9/♭13)}$ or a Dom.$^{7/♯5\ (9/♯11)}$ chord for example.

1 2 3 ♯4 ♯5 ♭7 8

3. Whole-Tone/Half-Tone Scale (WT/HT)

This eight-note scale is built by alternating whole steps and half steps.
Because of its symmetrical interval structure, there are only three different whole-tone/half-tone scales. The scale repeats itself in intervals of a minor third.
This scale doesn't contain a major third, which seems to somehow limit its possibilities. By harmonizing this scale with itself, you get a diminished seventh chord. This is exactly its main use: improvising over diminished chords or diminished seventh chords:

1 2 ♭3 4 ♭5 ♭6 6 7 8

4. Half-Tone/Whole-Tone Scale (HT/WT)

This scale is the "twin" of the whole-tone/half-tone scale. Like its "sister-scale" it consists of eight notes and repeats itself in intervals of a minor third. This scale contains the minor third, as well as the major third. Because it also contains the ♭7, ♭9, #9, #11 and 13, this is a wonderful scale to play over all kinds of chords from the dominant family. But the fun doesn't end here: this scale can also be used over many other chords.
Just try yourself.

1 ♭2 #2 3 #4 5 6 ♭7 8

III. CHARTS

ROOT C

Major Scale

Fingering   1   2   3   1   2   3   4   5

Minor Scales

Natural Minor

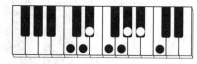

Fingering   1   2 3   1   23   4   5

Harmonic Minor

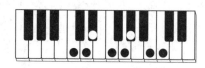

Fingering   1   2 3   1   23   4   5

Melodic Minor

Fingering   1   2 3   1   2   3   4   5

Ascending →

Fingering   1   2 3   1   23   4   5

← Descending

Chord Inversions

C Major

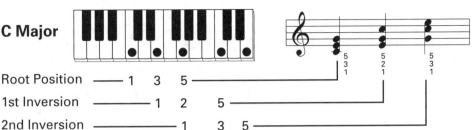

Root Position ——— 1   3   5 —————

1st Inversion ——— 1   2   5 —————

2nd Inversion ———— 1   3   5 —————

C Minor

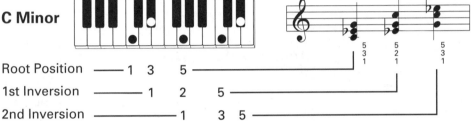

Root Position ——— 1   3   5 —————

1st Inversion ——— 1   2   5 —————

2nd Inversion ———— 1   3 5 —————

G Major
(Dominant/V)

F Major
(Subdominant/IV)

A Major
(Parallel Minor/VI)

Intervals

Harmonic Relationships

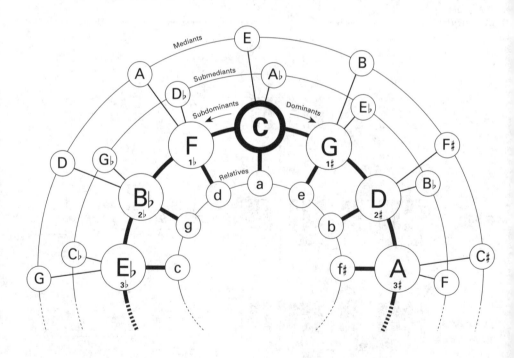

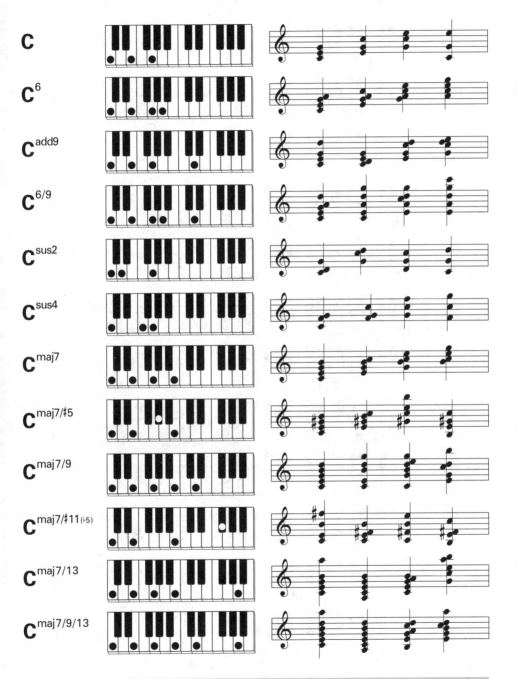

Major Chords

Minor Chords

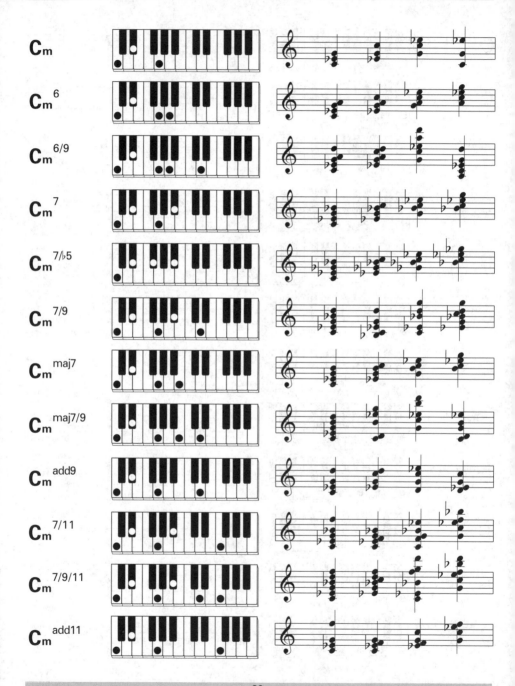

C_m

$C_m{}^6$

$C_m{}^{6/9}$

$C_m{}^7$

$C_m{}^{7/\flat 5}$

$C_m{}^{7/9}$

$C_m{}^{maj7}$

$C_m{}^{maj7/9}$

$C_m{}^{add9}$

$C_m{}^{7/11}$

$C_m{}^{7/9/11}$

$C_m{}^{add11}$

Seventh Chords

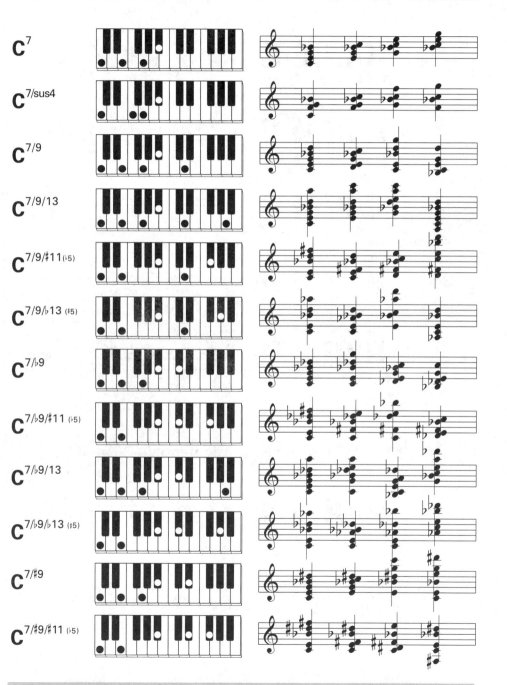

Seventh Chords

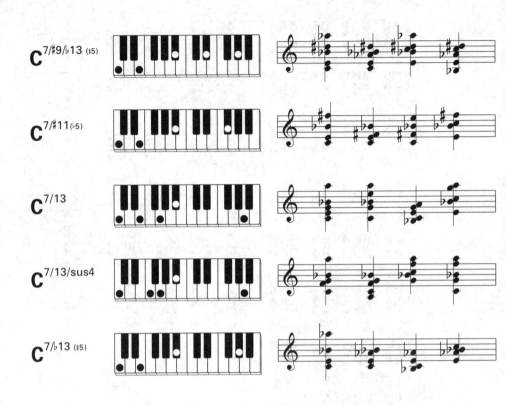

$C^{7/\sharp 9/\flat 13\ (\sharp 5)}$

$C^{7/\sharp 11\ (\flat 5)}$

$C^{7/13}$

$C^{7/13/sus4}$

$C^{7/\flat 13\ (\sharp 5)}$

Diminished & Augmented

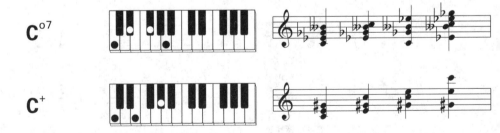

C^{o7}

C^{+}

Scales

Ionian

1 2 3 4 5 6 7 8

Dorian

1 2 ♭3 4 5 6 ♭7 8

Phrygian

1 ♭2 ♭3 4 5 ♭6 ♭7 8

Lydian

1 2 3 ♯4 5 6 7 8

Mixolydian
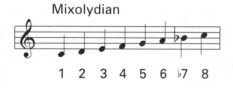

1 2 3 4 5 6 ♭7 8

Aeolian

1 2 ♭3 4 5 ♭6 ♭7 8

Locrian

1 ♭2 ♭3 4 ♭5 ♭6 ♭7 8

HM 3

1 2 3 4 ♯5 6 7 8

HM 5

1 ♭2 3 4 5 ♭6 ♭7 8

MM 7 / Altered

1 ♭2 ♯2 3 ♭5 ♯5 ♭7 8

Major Pentatonic
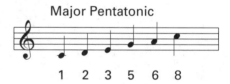

1 2 3 5 6 8

Minor Pentatonic

1 ♭3 4 5 ♭7 8

Blues Scale
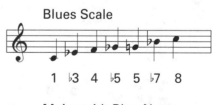

1 ♭3 4 ♭5 5 ♭7 8

Major with Blue Notes

1 2 ↓3 4 ↓5 6 ↓♭7 8

ROOT C♯/D♭

Major Scale

Fingering   2 3 1 2 3 4 1 2

Minor Scales

Natural Minor

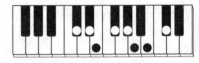

Fingering   2 3 1 2 3 1 2 3

Harmonic Minor

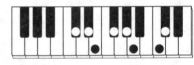

Fingering   2 3 1 2 3 1 2 3

Melodic Minor

Fingering   2 3 1 2 3 4 1 2

Ascending →

Fingering   2 3 1 2 3 4 1 2

← Descending

Chord Inversions

Db Major

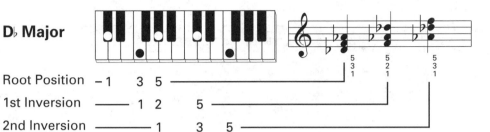

Root Position — 1   3   5 ——————————

1st Inversion ——— 1   2   5 ————

2nd Inversion ———————— 1   3   5 ——

Db Minor

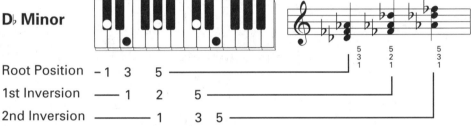

Root Position — 1   3   5 ——————

1st Inversion ——— 1   2   5 ————

2nd Inversion ———————— 1   3   5 ——

Ab Major
(Dominant/V)

Gb Major
(Subdominant/IV)

B Minor
(Parallel Minor/VI)

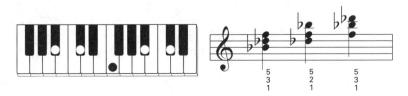

Intervals

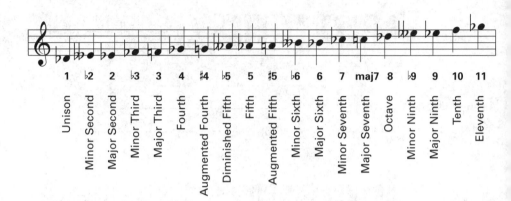

1	♭2	2	♭3	3	4	#4	♭5	5	#5	♭6	6	7	maj7	8	♭9	9	10	11
Unison	Minor Second	Major Second	Minor Third	Major Third	Fourth	Augmented Fourth	Diminished Fifth	Fifth	Augmented Fifth	Minor Sixth	Major Sixth	Minor Seventh	Major Seventh	Octave	Minor Ninth	Major Ninth	Tenth	Eleventh

Harmonic Relationships

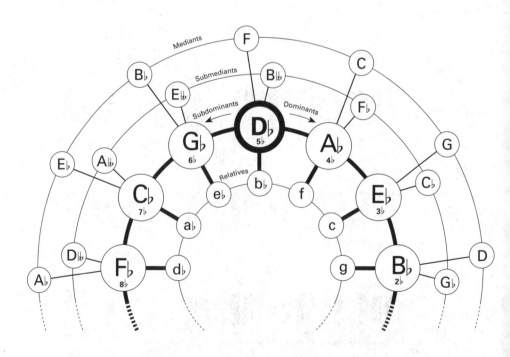

Major Chords

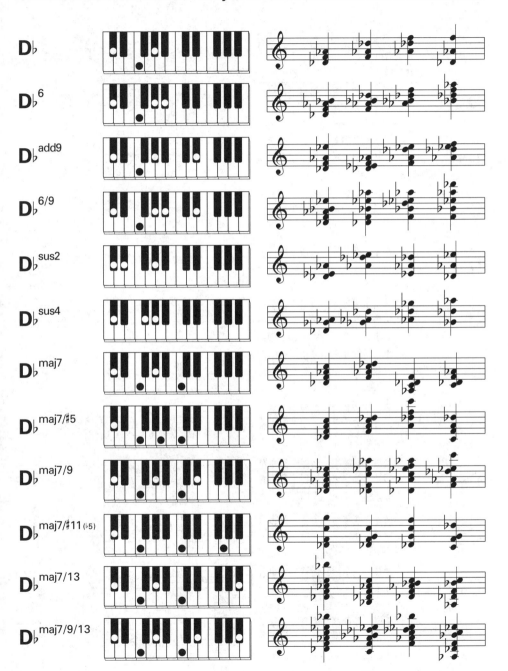

Db

Db 6

Db add9

Db 6/9

Db sus2

Db sus4

Db maj7

Db maj7/#5

Db maj7/9

Db maj7/#11 (b5)

Db maj7/13

Db maj7/9/13

Minor Chords

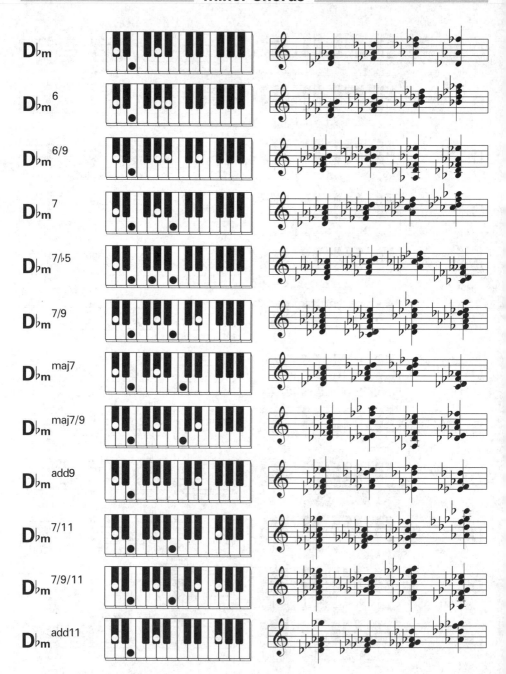

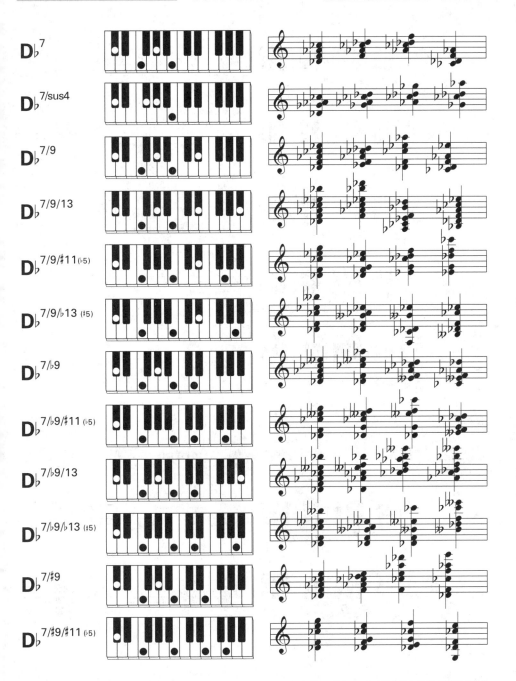

Seventh Chords

Seventh Chords

D♭ 7/#9/♭13 (#5)

D♭ 7/#11 (♭5)

D♭ 7/13

D♭ 7/13/sus4

D♭ 7/♭13 (#5)

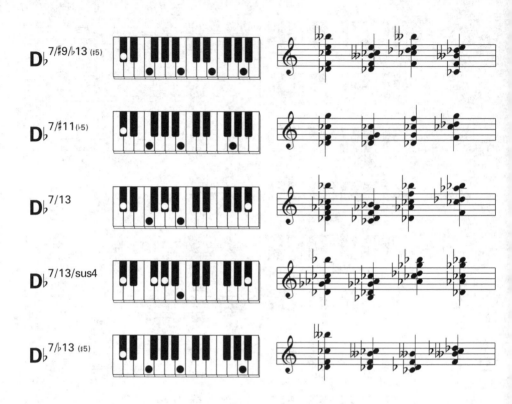

Diminished & Augmented

D♭ o7

D♭ +

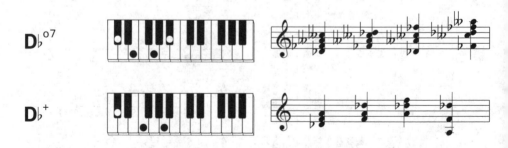

Scales

Ionian

1 2 3 4 5 6 7 8

Dorian

1 2 ♭3 4 5 6 ♭7 8

Phrygian

1 ♭2 ♭3 4 5 ♭6 ♭7 8

Lydian

1 2 3 #4 5 6 7 8

Mixolydian

1 2 3 4 5 6 ♭7 8

Aeolian

1 2 ♭3 4 5 ♭6 ♭7 8

Locrian

1 ♭2 ♭3 4 ♭5 ♭6 ♭7 8

HM 3

1 2 3 4 #5 6 7 8

HM 5

1 ♭2 3 4 5 ♭6 ♭7 8

MM 7 / Altered

1 ♭2 #2 3 ♭5 #5 ♭7 8

Major Pentatonic

1 2 3 5 6 8

Minor Pentatonic

1 ♭3 4 5 ♭7 8

Blues Scale

1 ♭3 4 ♭5 5 ♭7 8

Major with Blue Notes

1 2 ↓3 4 ↓5 6 ↓♭7 8

43

ROOT D

Major Scale

Fingering   1 2 3 1 2 3 4 5

Minor Scales

Natural Minor

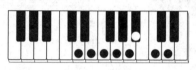

Fingering   1 2 3 1 2 3 4 5

Harmonic Minor

Fingering   1 2 3 1 2 3 4 5

Melodic Minor

Fingering   1 2 3 1 2 3 4 5

Ascending

Fingering   1 2 3 1 2 3 4 5

Descending

Chord Inversions

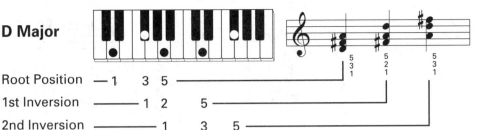

D Major

Root Position — 1   3   5
1st Inversion ——— 1 2   5
2nd Inversion ——— 1   3   5

D Minor

Root Position — 1   3   5
1st Inversion ——— 1 2   5
2nd Inversion ——— 1   3   5

A Major
(Dominant/V)

G Major
(Subdominant/IV)

B Minor
(Parallel Minor/VI)

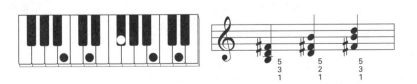

D

Intervals

Harmonic Relationships

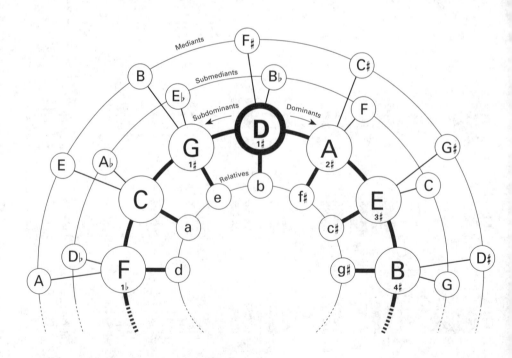

Major Chords

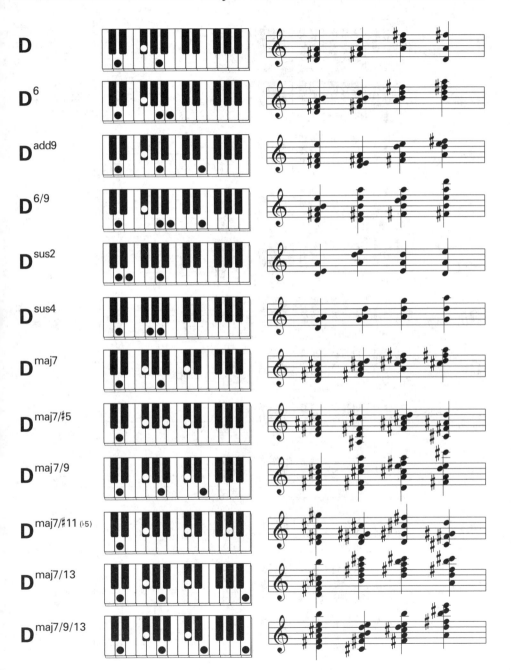

Minor Chords

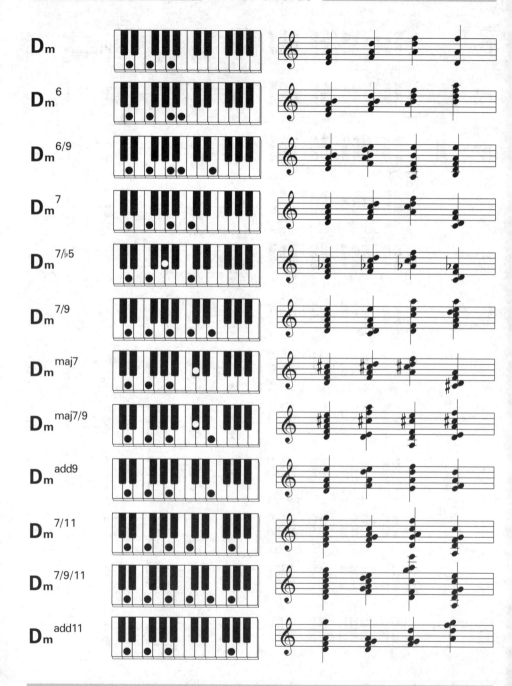

D_m

$D_m{}^6$

$D_m{}^{6/9}$

$D_m{}^7$

$D_m{}^{7/\flat 5}$

$D_m{}^{7/9}$

$D_m{}^{maj7}$

$D_m{}^{maj7/9}$

$D_m{}^{add9}$

$D_m{}^{7/11}$

$D_m{}^{7/9/11}$

$D_m{}^{add11}$

Seventh Chords

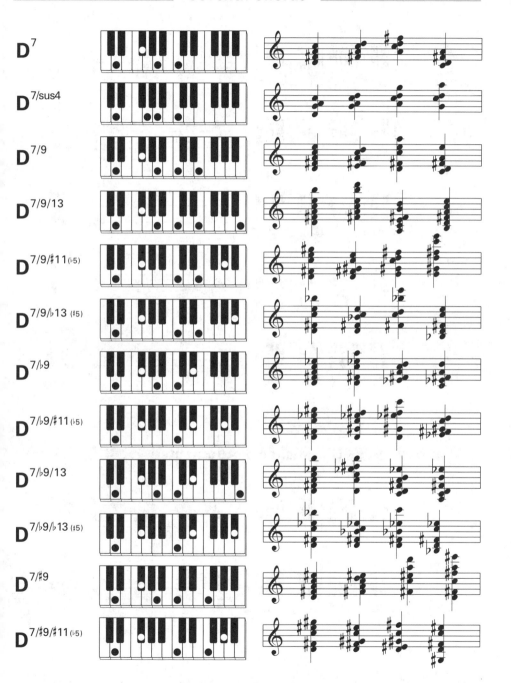

D^7

$D^{7/sus4}$

$D^{7/9}$

$D^{7/9/13}$

$D^{7/9/\#11(\flat5)}$

$D^{7/9/\flat13\,(\#5)}$

$D^{7/\flat9}$

$D^{7/\flat9/\#11(\flat5)}$

$D^{7/\flat9/13}$

$D^{7/\flat9/\flat13\,(\#5)}$

$D^{7/\#9}$

$D^{7/\#9/\#11(\flat5)}$

Seventh Chords

$D^{7/\#9/\flat13(\#5)}$

$D^{7/\#11(\flat5)}$

$D^{7/13}$

$D^{7/13/sus4}$

$D^{7/\flat13(\#5)}$

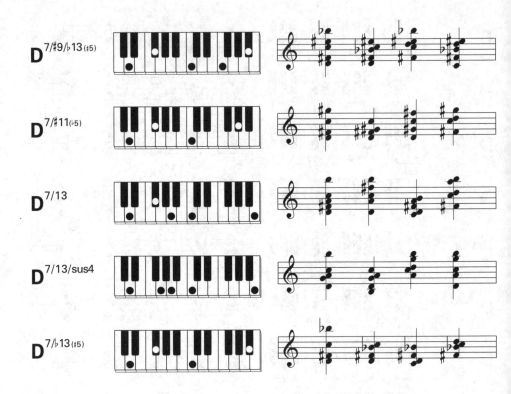

Diminished & Augmented

D^{o7}

D^{+}

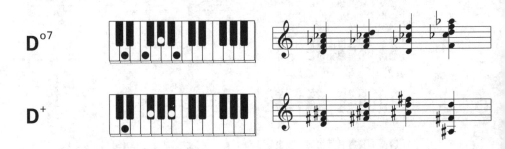

Scales

Ionian

1 2 3 4 5 6 7 8

Dorian

1 2 ♭3 4 5 6 ♭7 8

Phrygian

1 ♭2 ♭3 4 5 ♭6 ♭7 8

Lydian

1 2 3 ♯4 5 6 7 8

Mixolydian

1 2 3 4 5 6 ♭7 8

Aeolian

1 2 ♭3 4 5 ♭6 ♭7 8

Locrian

1 ♭2 ♭3 4 ♭5 ♭6 ♭7 8

HM 3

1 2 3 4 ♯5 6 7 8

HM 5

1 ♭2 3 4 5 ♭6 ♭7 8

MM 7 / Altered

1 ♭2 ♯2 3 ♭5 ♯5 ♭7 8

Major Pentatonic

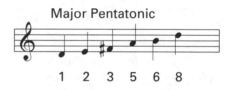

1 2 3 5 6 8

Minor Pentatonic

1 ♭3 4 5 ♭7 8

Blues Scale

1 ♭3 4 ♭5 5 ♭7 8

Major with Blue Notes

1 2 ↓3 4 ↓5 6 ↓♭7 8

ROOT D♯/E♭

Major Scale

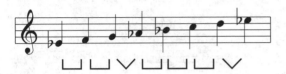

Fingering   2   1 2 3 4   1 2 3

Minor Scales

Natural Minor

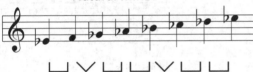

Fingering   2   1 2 3 4 1   2 3

Harmonic Minor

Fingering   2   1 2 3 4 1   2 3

Melodic Minor

Fingering   2   1 2 3 4   1 2 3
Ascending ⟶

Fingering   2   1 2 3 4 1   2 3
⟵ Descending

Chord Inversions

E♭ Major

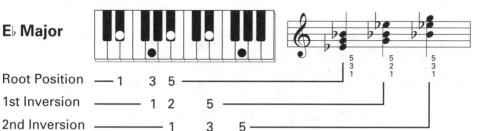

Root Position — 1   3   5
1st Inversion —   1 2   5
2nd Inversion —   1   3   5

E♭ Minor

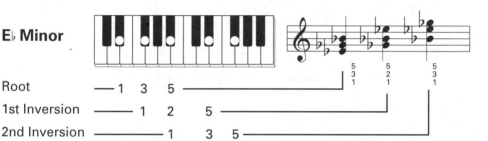

Root — 1   3   5
1st Inversion — 1 2   5
2nd Inversion — 1   3   5

B♭ Major
(Dominant/V)

A♭ Major
(Subdominant/IV)

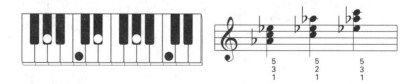

C Minor
(Parallel Minor/VI)

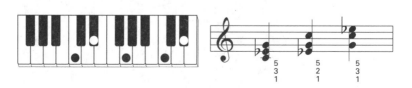

Intervals

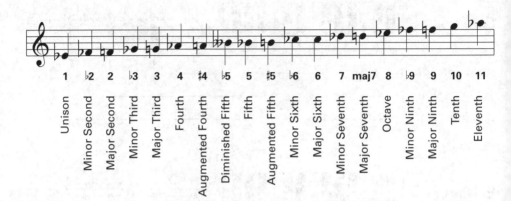

1	♭2	2	♭3	3	4	♯4	♭5	5	♯5	♭6	6	7	maj7	8	♭9	9	10	11

Unison · Minor Second · Major Second · Minor Third · Major Third · Fourth · Augmented Fourth · Diminished Fifth · Fifth · Augmented Fifth · Minor Sixth · Major Sixth · Minor Seventh · Major Seventh · Octave · Minor Ninth · Major Ninth · Tenth · Eleventh

Harmonic Relationships

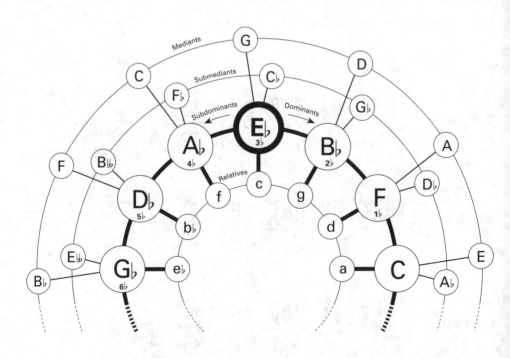

Major Chords

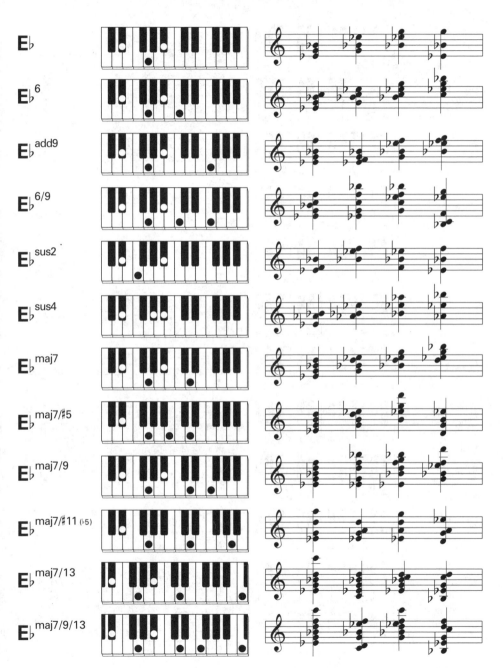

E♭

E♭6

E♭add9

E♭6/9

E♭sus2

E♭sus4

E♭maj7

E♭maj7/#5

E♭maj7/9

E♭maj7/#11 (♭5)

E♭maj7/13

E♭maj7/9/13

Minor Chords

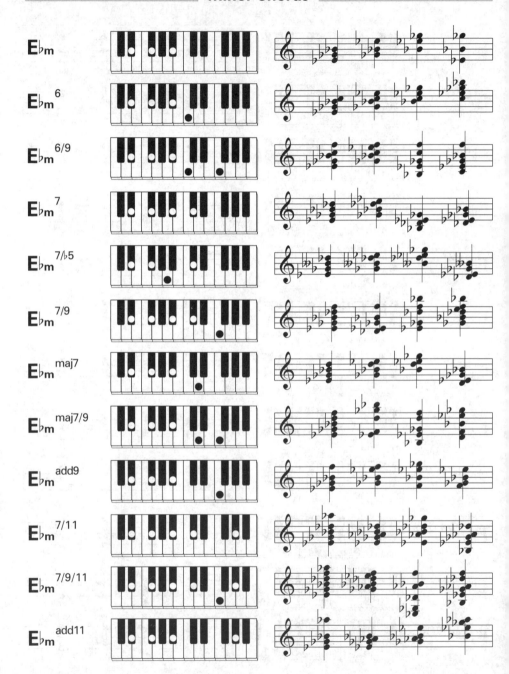

Seventh Chords

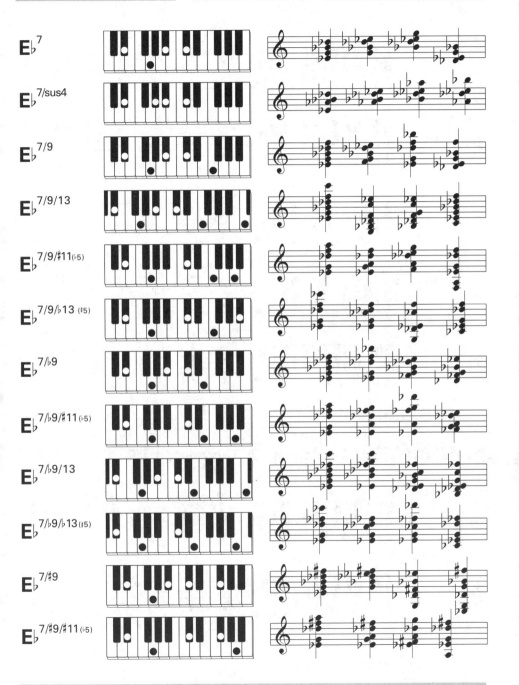

Seventh Chords

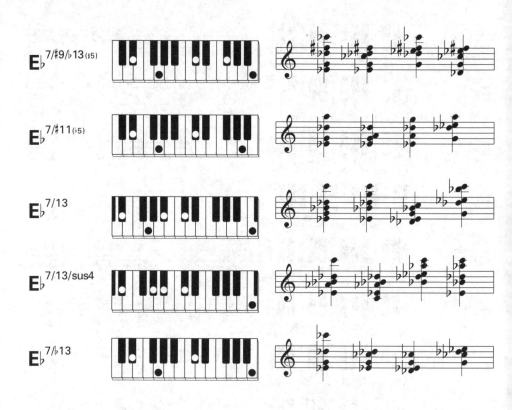

$E\flat^{7/\#9/\flat13(\natural5)}$

$E\flat^{7/\#11(\flat5)}$

$E\flat^{7/13}$

$E\flat^{7/13/sus4}$

$E\flat^{7/\flat13}$

Diminished & Augmented

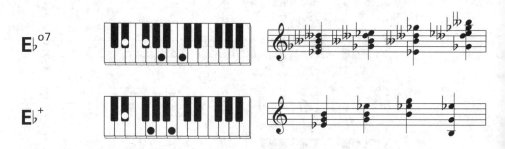

$E\flat^{o7}$

$E\flat^{+}$

Scales

Ionian

1 2 3 4 5 6 7 8

Dorian

1 2 ♭3 4 5 6 ♭7 8

Phrygian

1 ♭2 ♭3 4 5 ♭6 ♭7 8

Lydian

1 2 3 ♯4 5 6 7 8

Mixolydian

1 2 3 4 5 6 ♭7 8

Aeolian

1 2 ♭3 4 5 ♭6 ♭7 8

Locrian

1 ♭2 ♭3 4 ♭5 ♭6 ♭7 8

HM 3

1 2 3 4 ♯5 6 7 8

HM 5

1 ♭2 3 4 5 ♭6 ♭7 8

MM 7 / Altered

1 ♭2 ♯2 3 ♭5 ♯5 ♭7 8

Major Pentatonic

1 2 3 5 6 8

Minor Pentatonic

1 ♭3 4 5 ♭7 8

Blues Scale

1 ♭3 4 ♭5 5 ♭7 8

Major with Blue Notes

1 2 ↓3 4 ↓5 6 ↓♭7 8

ROOT E

Major Scale

Fingering 1 2 3 1 2 3 4 5

Minor Scales

Natural Minor

Fingering   1 2 3 1 2 3 4 5

Harmonic Minor

Fingering   1 2 3 1 2 3 4 5

Melodic Minor

Fingering   1 2 3 1 2 3 4 5

Ascending

Fingering   1 2 3 1 2 3 4 5

Descending

Chord Inversions

E Major

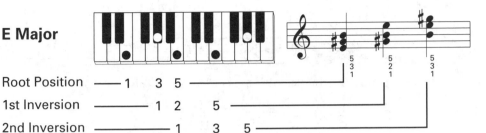

Root Position ——— 1   3   5 ———

1st Inversion ————— 1 2   5 ———

2nd Inversion ————— 1   3   5 ———

E Minor

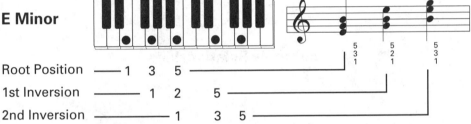

Root Position ——— 1   3   5 ———

1st Inversion ————— 1 2   5 ———

2nd Inversion ————— 1   3   5 ———

B Major
(Dominant/V)

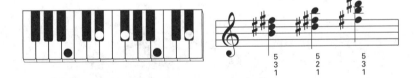

A Major
(Subdominant/IV)

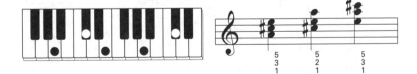

D♭ Minor
(Parallel Minor/VI)

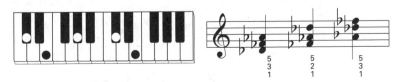

Intervals

1	b2	2	b3	3	4	#4	b5	5	#5	b6	6	7	maj7	8	b9	9	10	11

Unison — Minor Second — Major Second — Minor Third — Major Third — Fourth — Augmented Fourth — Diminished Fifth — Fifth — Augmented Fifth — Minor Sixth — Major Sixth — Minor Seventh — Major Seventh — Octave — Minor Ninth — Major Ninth — Tenth — Eleventh

Harmonic Relationships

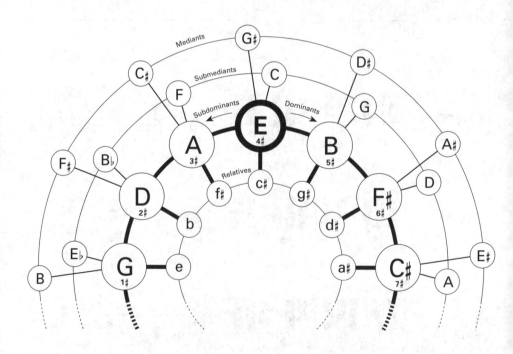

Major Chords

E
E⁶
E^{add9}
E^{6/9}
E^{sus2}
E^{sus4}
E^{maj7}
E^{maj7/#5}
E^{maj7/9}
E^{maj7/#11(♭5)}
E^{maj7/13}
E^{maj7/9/13}

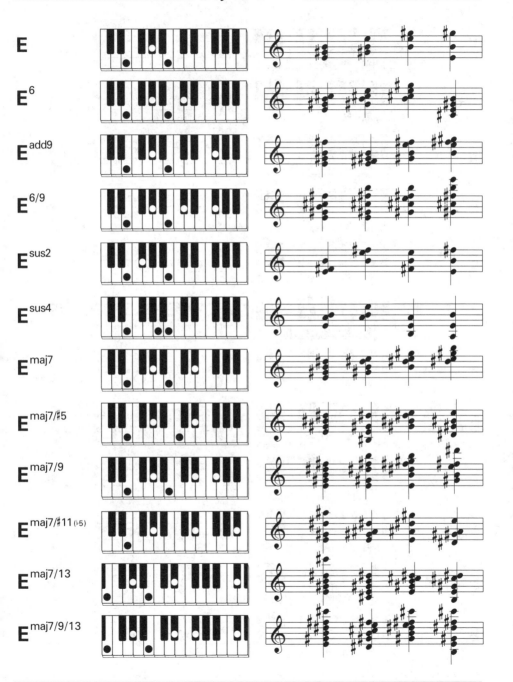

Minor Chords

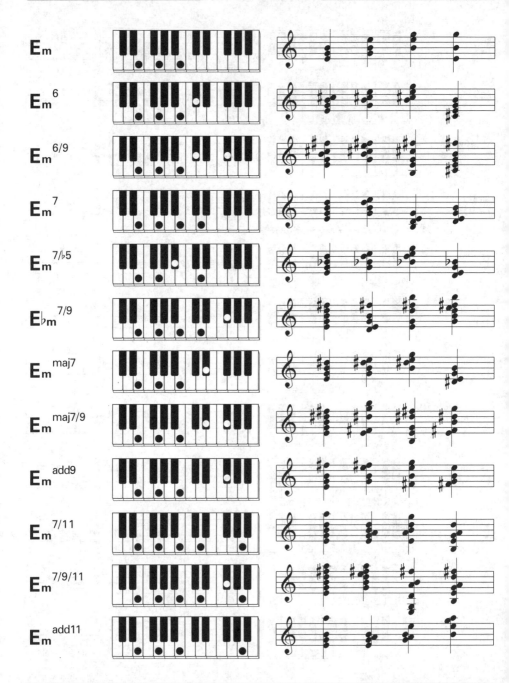

E_m

$E_m{}^6$

$E_m{}^{6/9}$

$E_m{}^7$

$E_m{}^{7/\flat 5}$

$E\flat_m{}^{7/9}$

$E_m{}^{maj7}$

$E_m{}^{maj7/9}$

$E_m{}^{add9}$

$E_m{}^{7/11}$

$E_m{}^{7/9/11}$

$E_m{}^{add11}$

Seventh Chords

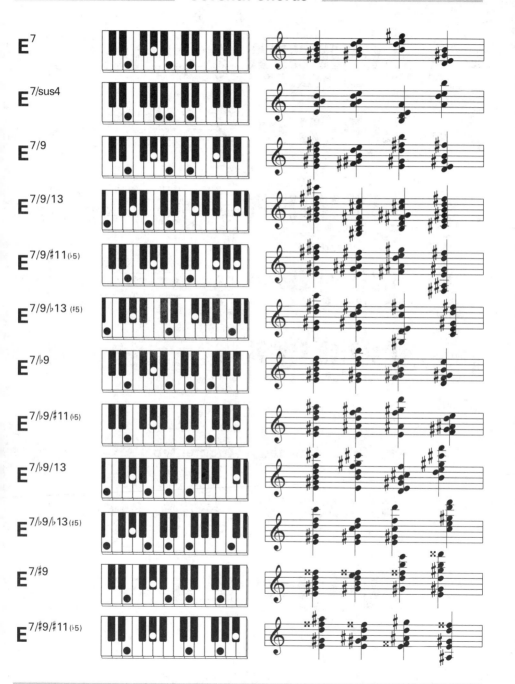

E^7	
$E^{7/sus4}$	
$E^{7/9}$	
$E^{7/9/13}$	
$E^{7/9/\#11(\flat 5)}$	
$E^{7/9/\flat 13\,(\#5)}$	
$E^{7/\flat 9}$	
$E^{7/\flat 9/\#11(\flat 5)}$	
$E^{7/\flat 9/13}$	
$E^{7/\flat 9/\flat 13(\#5)}$	
$E^{7/\#9}$	
$E^{7/\#9/\#11(\flat 5)}$	

Seventh Chords

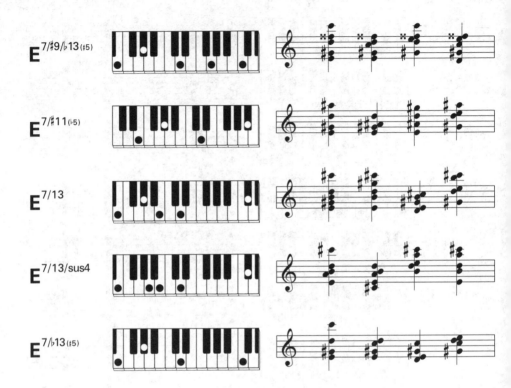

$E^{7/\sharp9/\flat13(\sharp5)}$

$E^{7/\sharp11(\flat5)}$

$E^{7/13}$

$E^{7/13/sus4}$

$E^{7/\flat13(\sharp5)}$

Diminished & Augmented

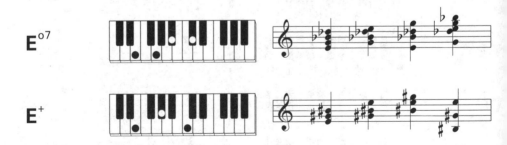

E^{o7}

E^{+}

Scales

Ionian

1 2 3 4 5 6 7 8

Dorian

1 2 ♭3 4 5 6 ♭7 8

Phrygian

1 ♭2 ♭3 4 5 ♭6 ♭7 8

Lydian

1 2 3 ♯4 5 6 7 8

Mixolydian

1 2 3 4 5 6 ♭7 8

Aeolian

1 2 ♭3 4 5 ♭6 ♭7 8

Locrian

1 ♭2 ♭3 4 ♭5 ♭6 ♭7 8

HM 3

1 2 3 4 ♯5 6 7 8

HM 5

1 ♭2 3 4 5 ♭6 ♭7 8

MM 7 / Altered

1 ♭2 ♯2 3 ♭5 ♯5 ♭7 8

Major Pentatonic

1 2 3 5 6 8

Minor Pentatonic

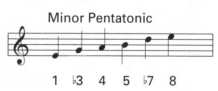

1 ♭3 4 5 ♭7 8

Blues Scale

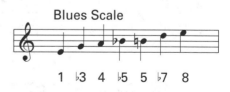

1 ♭3 4 ♭5 5 ♭7 8

Major with Blue Notes

1 2 ↓3 4 ↓5 6 ↓♭7 8

ROOT F

Major Scale

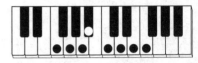

Fingering 1 2 3 4 1 2 3 4

Minor Scales

Natural Minor

Fingering 1 2 3 4 1 2 3 4

Harmonic Minor

Fingering 1 2 3 4 1 2 3 4

Melodic Minor

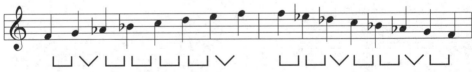

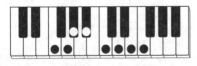

Fingering 1 2 3 4 1 2 3 4

Ascending →

Fingering 1 2 3 4 1 2 3 4

← Descending

Chord Inversions

F Major

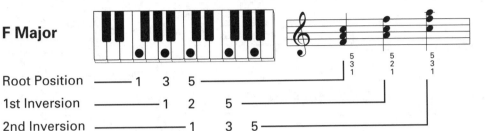

Root Position ——— 1   3   5 ———————————

1st Inversion ——————— 1   2   5 ———————

2nd Inversion ————————— 1   3   5 ————

F Minor

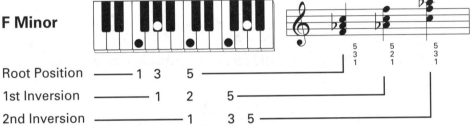

Root Position ——— 1   3   5 ———————————

1st Inversion ——————— 1   2   5 —————

2nd Inversion ———————————— 1   3   5 ————

C Major
(Dominant/V)

B♭ Major
(Subdominant/IV)

D Minor
(Parallel Minor/VI)

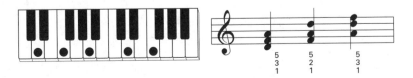

Intervals

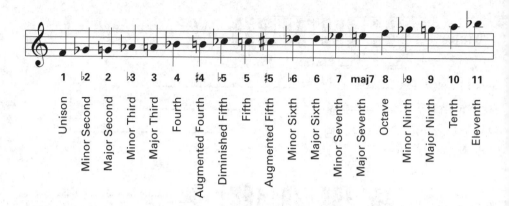

Harmonic Relationships

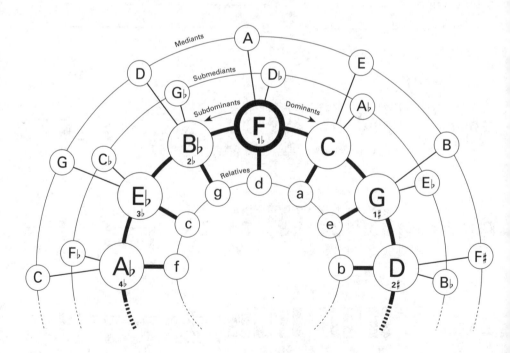

Major Chords

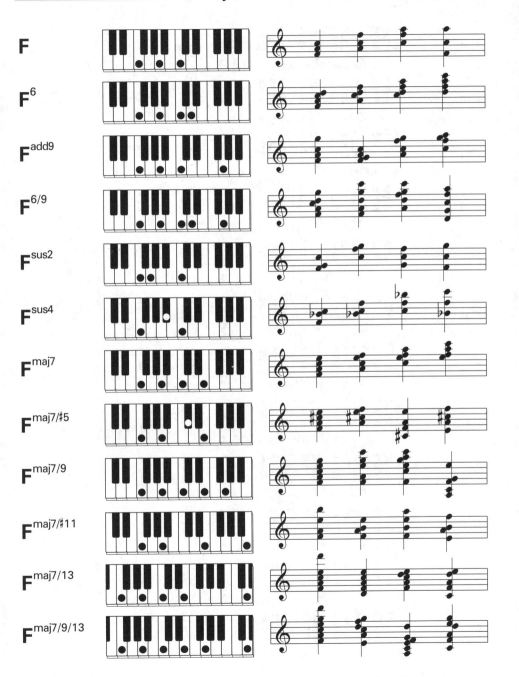

Minor Chords

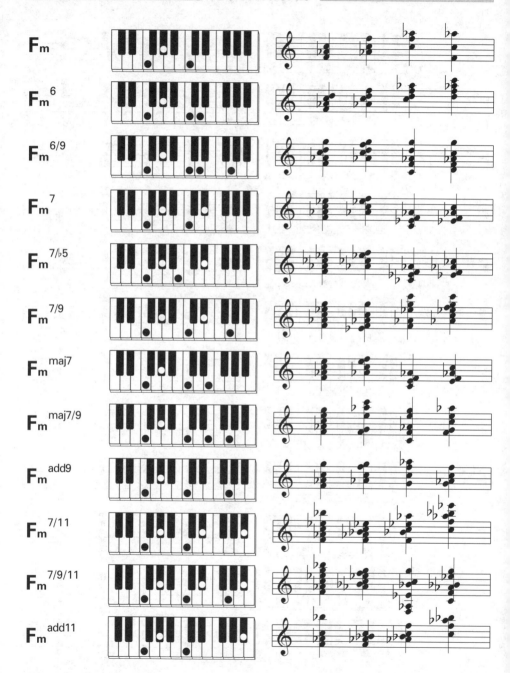

Seventh Chords

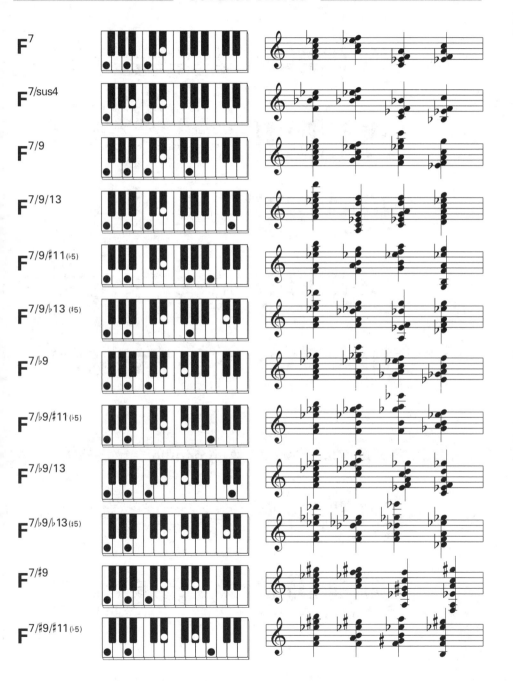

Seventh Chords

F$^{7/\sharp 9/\flat 13(\sharp 5)}$

F$^{7/\sharp 11(\flat 5)}$

F$^{7/13}$

F$^{7/13/sus4}$

F$^{7/\flat 13(\sharp 5)}$

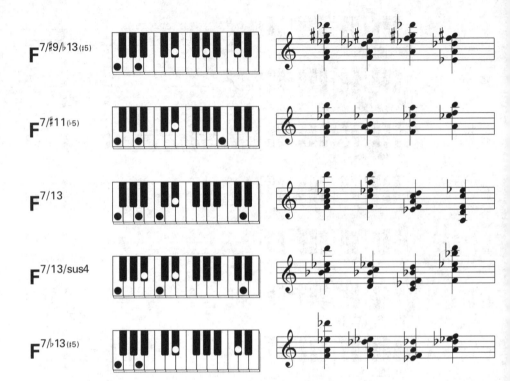

Diminished & Augmented

F^{o7}

F^{+}

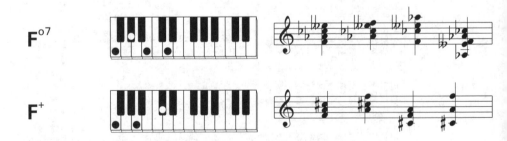

Scales

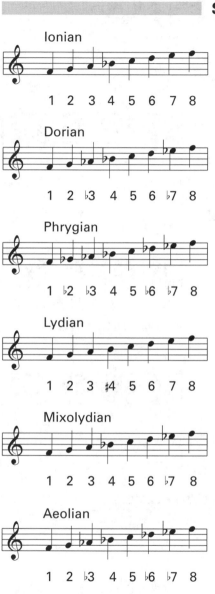

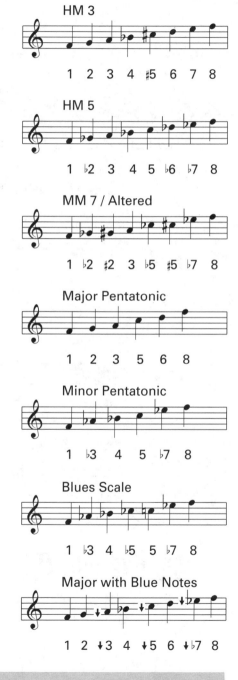

Ionian

1 2 3 4 5 6 7 8

Dorian

1 2 ♭3 4 5 6 ♭7 8

Phrygian

1 ♭2 ♭3 4 5 ♭6 ♭7 8

Lydian

1 2 3 ♯4 5 6 7 8

Mixolydian

1 2 3 4 5 6 ♭7 8

Aeolian

1 2 ♭3 4 5 ♭6 ♭7 8

Locrian

1 ♭2 ♭3 4 ♭5 ♭6 ♭7 8

HM 3

1 2 3 4 ♯5 6 7 8

HM 5

1 ♭2 3 4 5 ♭6 ♭7 8

MM 7 / Altered

1 ♭2 ♯2 3 ♭5 ♯5 ♭7 8

Major Pentatonic

1 2 3 5 6 8

Minor Pentatonic

1 ♭3 4 5 ♭7 8

Blues Scale

1 ♭3 4 ♭5 5 ♭7 8

Major with Blue Notes

1 2 ↓3 4 ↓5 6 ↓♭7 8

ROOT F♯/G♭

Major Scale

Fingering   2 3 4 1   2 3 1   2

Minor Scales

Natural Minor

Fingering   2 3 1 2   3 1 2   3

Harmonic Minor

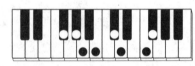

Fingering   2 3 1 2   3 1   2 3

Melodic Minor

Fingering   2 3 1 2   3 4   1 2

Ascending →

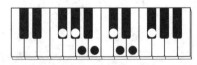

Fingering   2 3 1 2   3 1 2   3

← Descending

Chord Inversions

F# Major

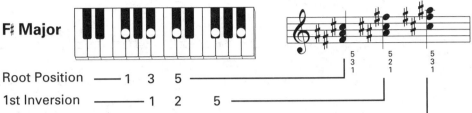

Root Position —— 1   3   5 ——————
1st Inversion ———— 1   2   5 ——————
2nd Inversion ———————— 1   3   5 ——————

F# Minor

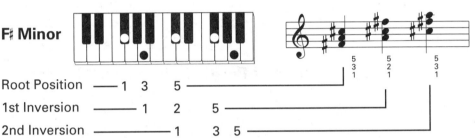

Root Position —— 1   3   5 ——————
1st Inversion ———— 1   2   5 ——————
2nd Inversion ———————— 1   3   5 ——————

C# Major
(Dominant/V)

B Major
(Subdominant/IV)

D# Minor
(Parallel Minor/VI)

Intervals

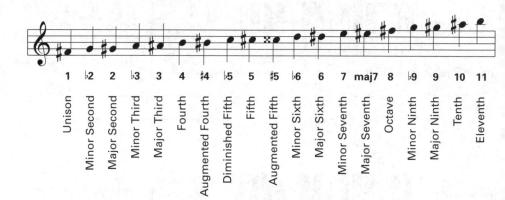

1	♭2	2	♭3	3	4	♯4	♭5	5	♯5	♭6	6	7	maj7	8	♭9	9	10	11
Unison	Minor Second	Major Second	Minor Third	Major Third	Fourth	Augmented Fourth	Diminished Fifth	Fifth	Augmented Fifth	Minor Sixth	Major Sixth	Minor Seventh	Major Seventh	Octave	Minor Ninth	Major Ninth	Tenth	Eleventh

Harmonic Relationships

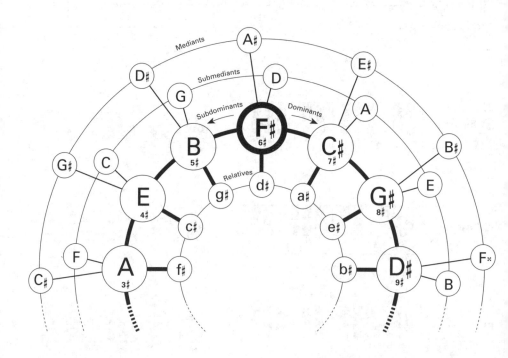

Major Chords

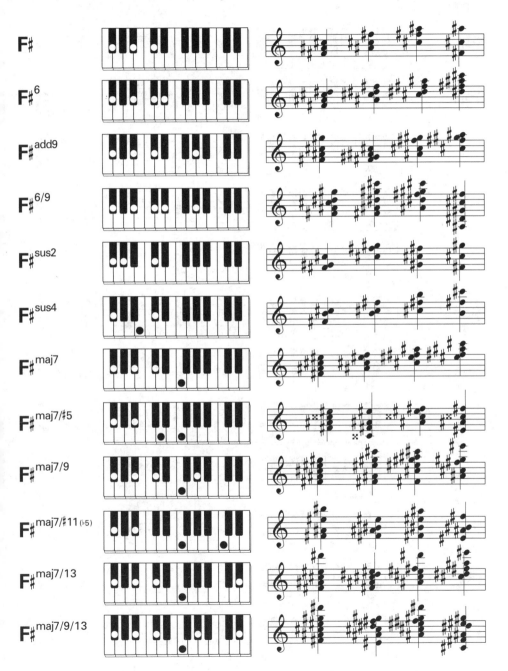

F#

F#6

F#add9

F#6/9

F#sus2

F#sus4

F#maj7

F#maj7/#5

F#maj7/9

F#maj7/#11(b5)

F#maj7/13

F#maj7/9/13

Minor Chords

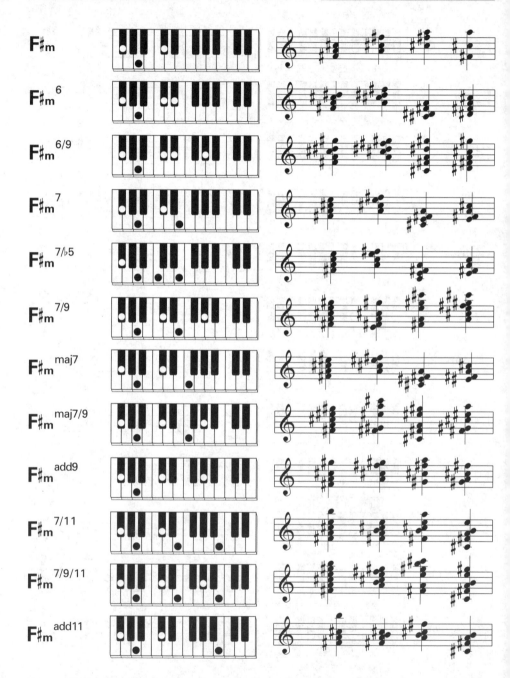

F♯m

F♯m⁶

F♯m⁶/⁹

F♯m⁷

F♯m⁷/♭⁵

F♯m⁷/⁹

F♯mᵐᵃʲ⁷

F♯mᵐᵃʲ⁷/⁹

F♯mᵃᵈᵈ⁹

F♯m⁷/¹¹

F♯m⁷/⁹/¹¹

F♯mᵃᵈᵈ¹¹

Seventh Chords

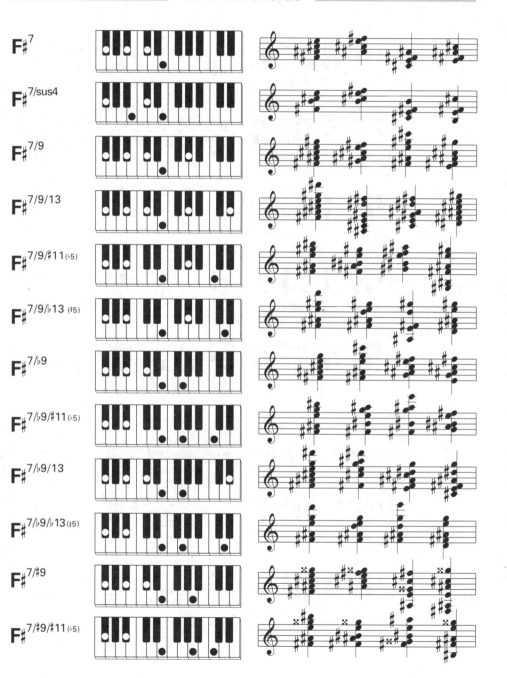

Seventh Chords

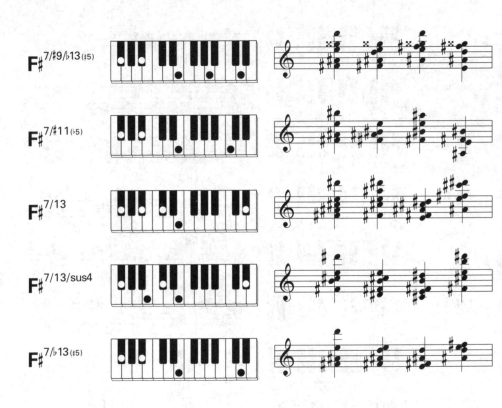

Diminished & Augmented

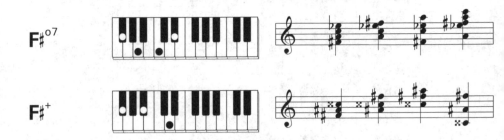

Scales

Ionian

1 2 3 4 5 6 7 8

Dorian

1 2 b3 4 5 6 b7 8

Phrygian

1 b2 b3 4 5 b6 b7 8

Lydian

1 2 3 #4 5 6 7 8

Mixolydian

1 2 3 4 5 6 b7 8

Aeolian

1 2 b3 4 5 b6 b7 8

Locrian

1 b2 b3 4 b5 b6 b7 8

HM 3

1 2 3 4 #5 6 7 8

HM 5

1 b2 3 4 5 b6 b7 8

MM 7 / Altered

1 b2 #2 3 b5 #5 b7 8

Major Pentatonic

1 2 3 5 6 8

Minor Pentatonic

1 b3 4 5 b7 8

Blues Scale

1 b3 4 b5 5 b7 8

Major with Blue Notes
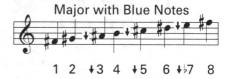

1 2 ↓3 4 ↓5 6 ↓b7 8

ROOT G

Major Scale

Fingering   1 2 3 1 2 3 4 5

Minor Scales

Natural Minor

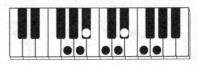

Fingering   1 2 3 1 2 3 4 5

Harmonic Minor

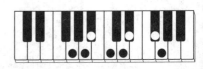

Fingering   1 2 3 1 2 3   4 5

Melodic Minor

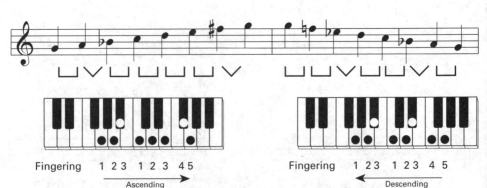

Fingering   1 2 3   1 2 3   4 5
Ascending →

Fingering   1 2 3   1 2 3   4 5
← Descending

Chord Inversions

G Major

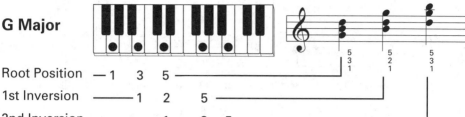

Root Position — 1 3 5
1st Inversion —— 1 2 5
2nd Inversion ——— 1 3 5

G Minor

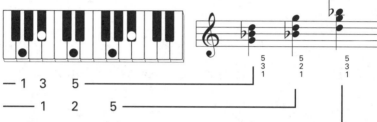

Root Position — 1 3 5
1st Inversion —— 1 2 5
2nd Inversion ——— 1 3 5

D Major
(Dominant/V)

C Major
(Subdominant/IV)

E Minor
(Parallel Minor/VI)

Intervals

1	♭2	2	♭3	3	4	#4	♭5	5	#5	♭6	6	7	maj7	8	♭9	9	10	11
Unison	Minor Second	Major Second	Minor Third	Major Third	Fourth	Augmented Fourth	Diminished Fifth	Fifth	Augmented Fifth	Minor Sixth	Major Sixth	Minor Seventh	Major Seventh	Octave	Minor Ninth	Major Ninth	Tenth	Eleventh

Harmonic Relationships

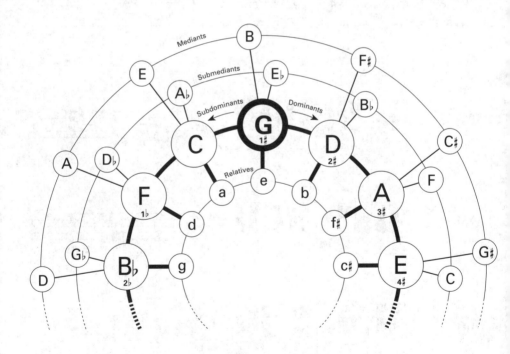

Major Chords

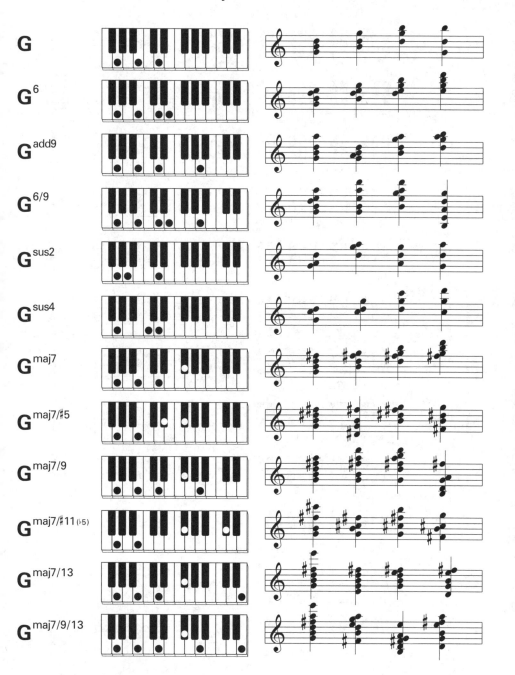

G

Minor Chords

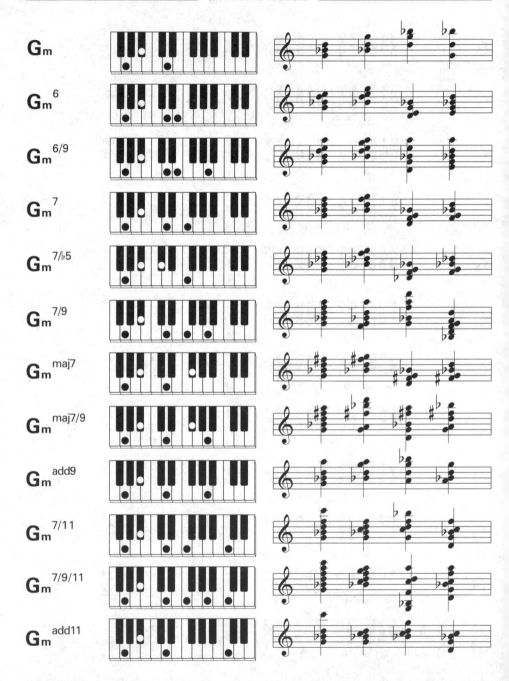

Gm

Gm⁶

Gm^{6/9}

Gm⁷

Gm^{7/♭5}

Gm^{7/9}

Gm^{maj7}

Gm^{maj7/9}

Gm^{add9}

Gm^{7/11}

Gm^{7/9/11}

Gm^{add11}

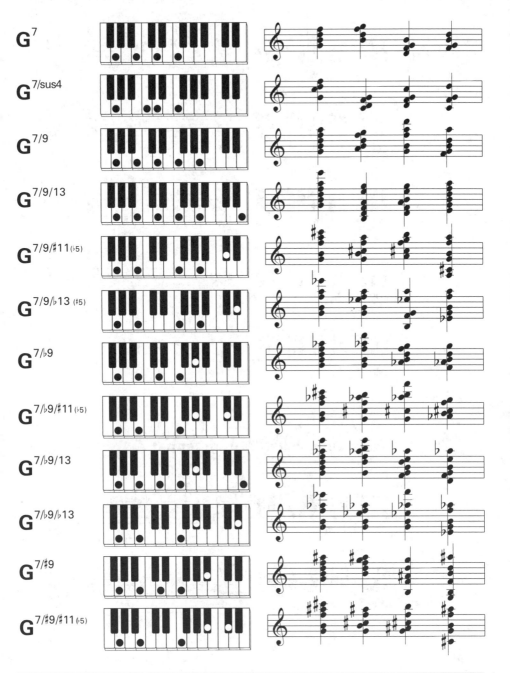

Seventh Chords

Seventh Chords

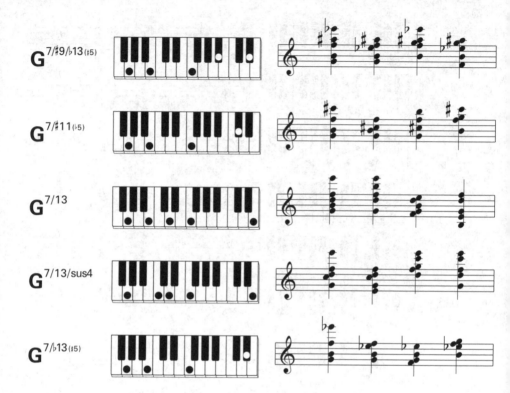

$G^{7/\sharp 9/\flat 13(\sharp 5)}$

$G^{7/\sharp 11(\flat 5)}$

$G^{7/13}$

$G^{7/13/sus4}$

$G^{7/\flat 13(\sharp 5)}$

Diminished & Augmented

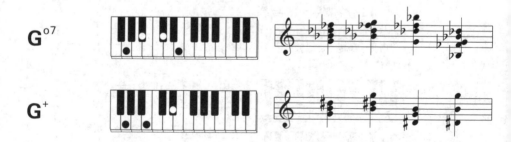

G^{o7}

G^{+}

Scales

Ionian

1 2 3 4 5 6 7 8

Dorian

1 2 ♭3 4 5 6 ♭7 8

Phrygian

1 ♭2 ♭3 4 5 ♭6 ♭7 8

Lydian

1 2 3 ♯4 5 6 7 8

Mixolydian

1 2 3 4 5 6 ♭7 8

Aeolian

1 2 ♭3 4 5 ♭6 ♭7 8

Locrian

1 ♭2 ♭3 4 ♭5 ♭6 ♭7 8

HM 3

1 2 3 4 ♯5 6 7 8

HM 5

1 ♭2 3 4 5 ♭6 ♭7 8

MM 7 / Altered

1 ♭2 ♯2 3 ♭5 ♯5 ♭7 8

Major Pentatonic

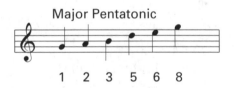

1 2 3 5 6 8

Minor Pentatonic

1 ♭3 4 5 ♭7 8

Blues Scale

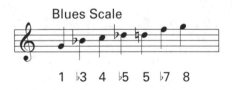

1 ♭3 4 ♭5 5 ♭7 8

Major with Blue Notes

1 2 ↓3 4 ↓5 6 ↓♭7 8

ROOT G♯/A♭

Major Scale

Fingering   2 3   1 2 3   1 2 3

Minor Scales

Natural Minor

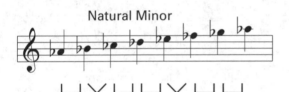

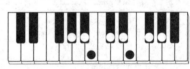

Fingering   2 3 1   2 3 1   2 3

Harmonic Minor

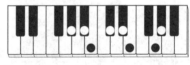

Fingering   2 3 1   2 3 1   2 3

Melodic Minor

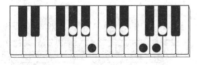

Fingering   2 3 1   2 3   1 2 3

Ascending

Fingering   2 3 1   2 3 1   2 3

Descending

Chold Inversions

A♭ Major

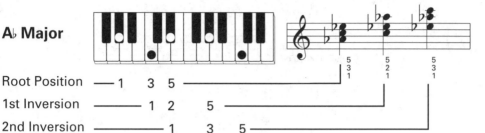

Root Position — 1 3 5 ————————————————

1st Inversion ——— 1 2   5 ————————————

2nd Inversion ————— 1 3   5 —————————

A♭ Minor

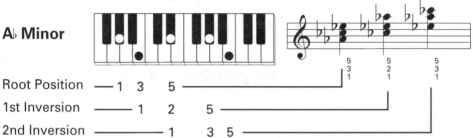

Root Position — 1 3   5 ———————————————

1st Inversion ——— 1 2   5 ————————————

2nd Inversion ————— 1 3 5 ————————————

E♭ Major
(Dominant/V)

D♭ Major
(Subdominant/IV)

F Minor
(Parallel Minor/VI)

Intervals

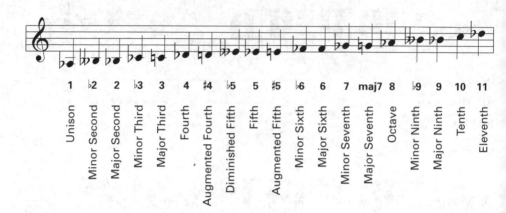

1	♭2	2	♭3	3	4	♯4	♭5	5	♯5	♭6	6	7	maj7	8	♭9	9	10	11
Unison	Minor Second	Major Second	Minor Third	Major Third	Fourth	Augmented Fourth	Diminished Fifth	Fifth	Augmented Fifth	Minor Sixth	Major Sixth	Minor Seventh	Major Seventh	Octave	Minor Ninth	Major Ninth	Tenth	Eleventh

Harmonic Relationships

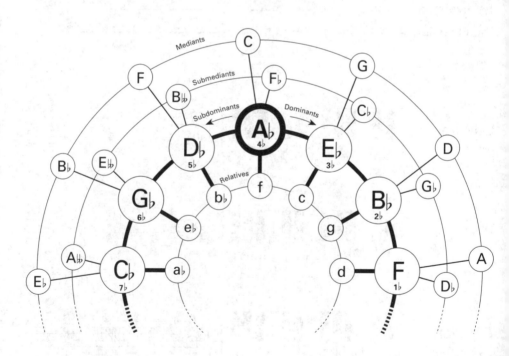

Major Chords

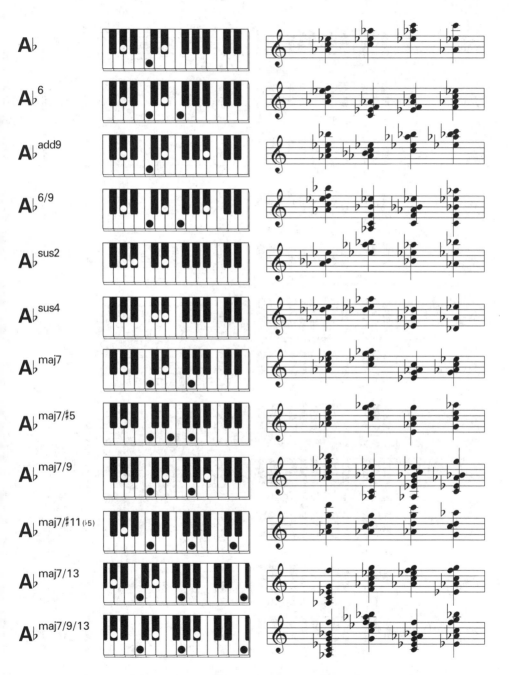

Minor Chords

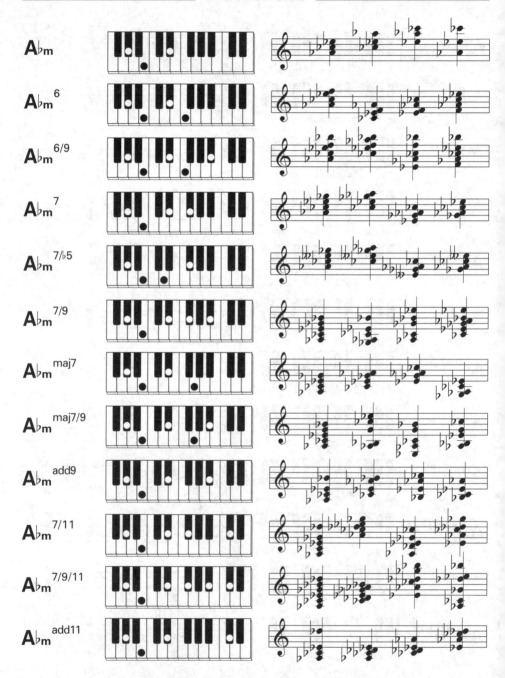

Abm

Abm 6

Abm 6/9

Abm 7

Abm 7/b5

Abm 7/9

Abm maj7

Abm maj7/9

Abm add9

Abm 7/11

Abm 7/9/11

Abm add11

Seventh Chords

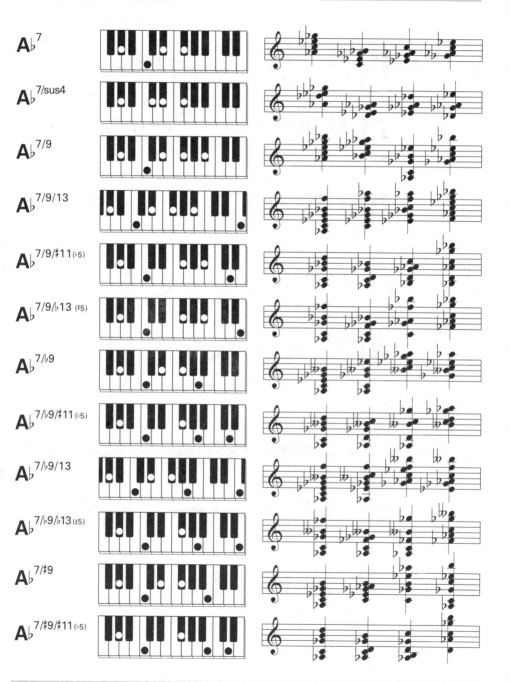

Seventh Chords

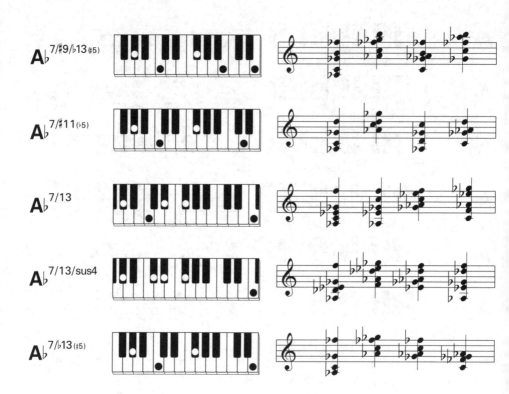

$A♭^{7/\sharp9/♭13(\sharp5)}$

$A♭^{7/\sharp11(♭5)}$

$A♭^{7/13}$

$A♭^{7/13/sus4}$

$A♭^{7/♭13(\sharp5)}$

Diminished & Augmented

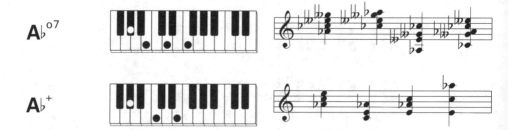

$A♭^{o7}$

$A♭^{+}$

Scales

Ionian

1 2 3 4 5 6 7 8

Dorian

1 2 ♭3 4 5 6 ♭7 8

Phrygian

1 ♭2 ♭3 4 5 ♭6 ♭7 8

Lydian

1 2 3 ♯4 5 6 7 8

Mixolydian

1 2 3 4 5 6 ♭7 8

Aeolian

1 2 ♭3 4 5 ♭6 ♭7 8

Locrian

1 ♭2 ♭3 4 ♭5 ♭6 ♭7 8

HM 3

1 2 3 4 ♯5 6 7 8

HM 5

1 ♭2 3 4 5 ♭6 ♭7 8

MM 7 / Altered

1 ♭2 ♯2 3 ♭5 ♯5 ♭7 8

Major Pentatonic

1 2 3 5 6 8

Minor Pentatonic

1 ♭3 4 5 ♭7 8

Blues Scale

1 ♭3 4 ♭5 5 ♭7 8

Major with Blue Notes

1 2 ↓3 4 ↓5 6 ↓7 8

ROOT A

Major Scale

Fingering 1 2 31 2 3 4 5

Minor Scales

Natural Minor

Fingering 1 2 3 1 2 3 4 5

Harmonic Minor

Fingering 1 2 3 1 2 3 4 5

Melodic Minor

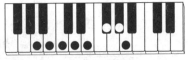

Fingering 1 2 3 1 2 3 4 5

Ascending →

Fingering 1 2 3 1 2 3 4 5

← Descending

Chord Inversions

A Major

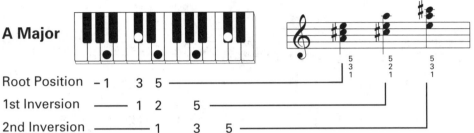

Root Position	– 1	3	5
1st Inversion	1	2	5
2nd Inversion	1	3	5

A Minor

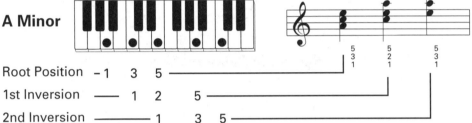

Root Position	– 1	3	5
1st Inversion	1	2	5
2nd Inversion	1	3	5

E Major
(Dominant/V)

D Major
(Subdominant/IV)

F♯ Minor
(Parallel Minor/VI)

Intervals

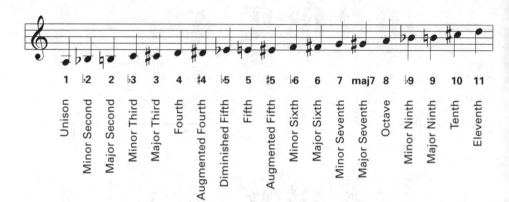

1	♭2	2	♭3	3	4	#4	♭5	5	#5	♭6	6	7	maj7	8	♭9	9	10	11
Unison	Minor Second	Major Second	Minor Third	Major Third	Fourth	Augmented Fourth	Diminished Fifth	Fifth	Augmented Fifth	Minor Sixth	Major Sixth	Minor Seventh	Major Seventh	Octave	Minor Ninth	Major Ninth	Tenth	Eleventh

Harmonic Relationships

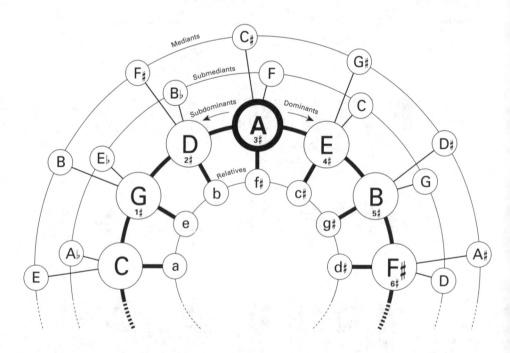

Major Chords

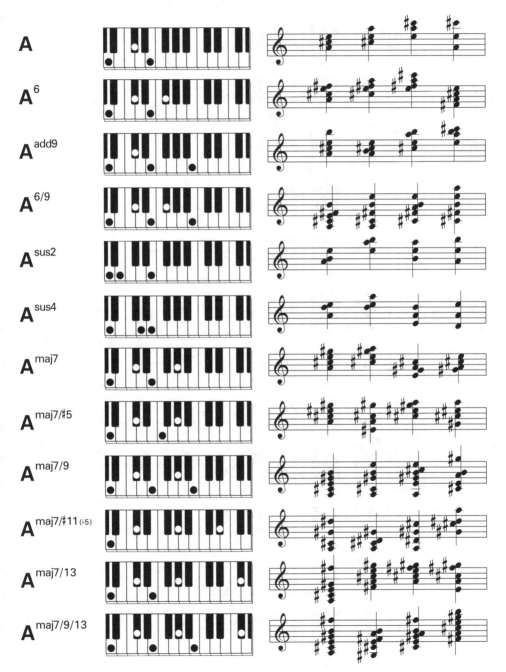

A

A⁶

Aᵃᵈᵈ⁹

A⁶ᐟ⁹

Aˢᵘˢ²

Aˢᵘˢ⁴

Aᵐᵃʲ⁷

Aᵐᵃʲ⁷ᐟ♯⁵

Aᵐᵃʲ⁷ᐟ⁹

Aᵐᵃʲ⁷ᐟ♯¹¹⁽♭⁵⁾

Aᵐᵃʲ⁷ᐟ¹³

Aᵐᵃʲ⁷ᐟ⁹ᐟ¹³

Minor Chords

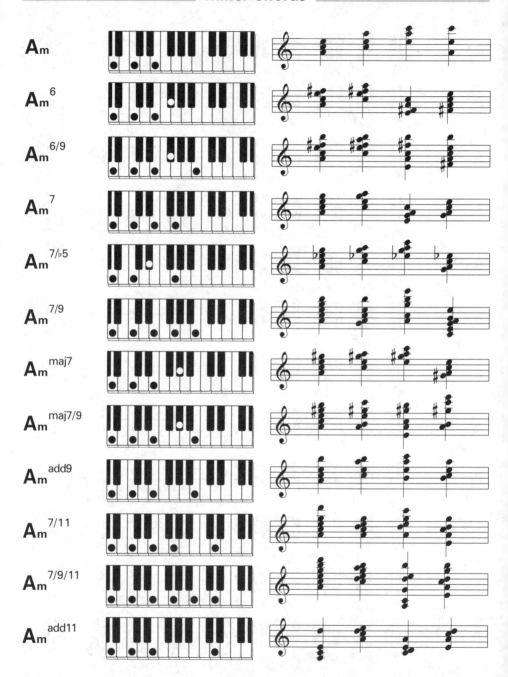

Seventh Chords

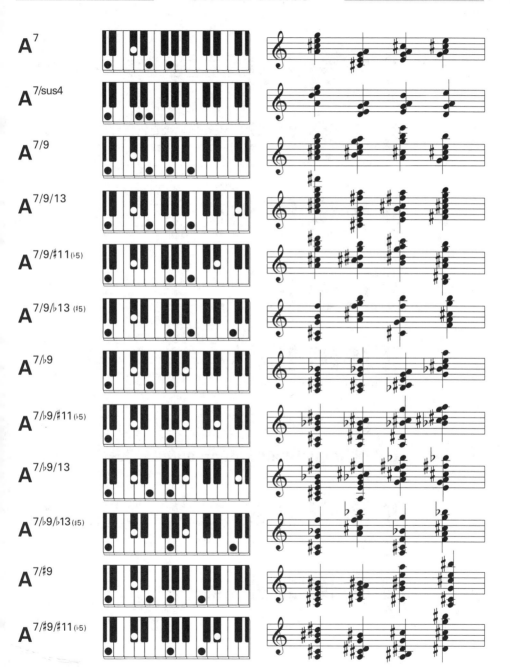

A⁷

A⁷/sus4

A⁷/⁹

A⁷/⁹/¹³

A⁷/⁹/♯¹¹(♭⁵)

A⁷/⁹/♭¹³(♯⁵)

A⁷/♭⁹

A⁷/♭⁹/♯¹¹(♭⁵)

A⁷/♭⁹/¹³

A⁷/♭⁹/♭¹³(♯⁵)

A⁷/♯⁹

A⁷/♯⁹/♯¹¹(♭⁵)

Seventh Chords

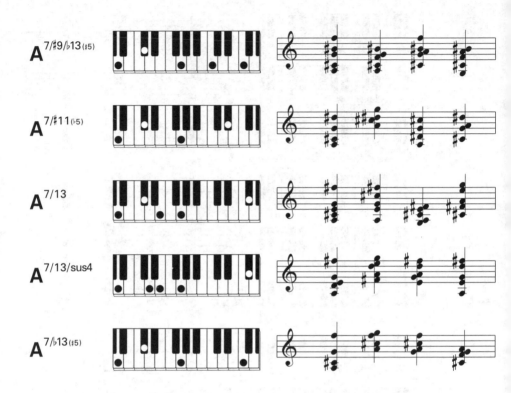

$A^{7/\sharp9/\flat13\,(\sharp5)}$

$A^{7/\sharp11\,(\flat5)}$

$A^{7/13}$

$A^{7/13/sus4}$

$A^{7/\flat13\,(\sharp5)}$

Diminished & Augmented

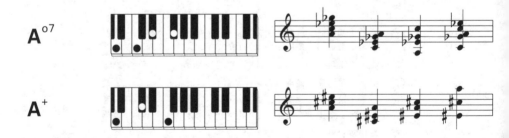

A^{o7}

A^{+}

Scales

Ionian

1 2 3 4 5 6 7 8

Dorian

1 2 ♭3 4 5 6 ♭7 8

Phrygian

1 ♭2 ♭3 4 5 ♭6 ♭7 8

Lydian

1 2 3 ♯4 5 6 7 8

Mixolydian

1 2 3 4 5 6 ♭7 8

Aeolian

1 2 ♭3 4 5 ♭6 ♭7 8

Locrian

1 ♭2 ♭3 4 ♭5 ♭6 ♭7 8

HM 3

1 2 3 4 ♯5 6 7 8

HM 5

1 ♭2 3 4 5 ♭6 ♭7 8

MM 7 / Altered

1 ♭2 ♯2 3 ♭5 ♯5 ♭7 8

Major Pentatonic

1 2 3 5 6 8

Minor Pentatonic

1 ♭3 4 5 ♭7 8

Blues Scale

1 ♭3 4 ♭5 5 ♭7 8

Major with Blue Notes

1 2 ↓3 4 ↓5 6 ↓♭7 8

ROOT A♯/B♭

Major Scale

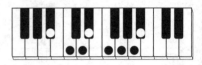

Fingering   2   1 23   1 2 3 4

Minor Scales

Natural Minor

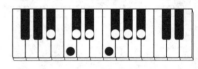

Fingering   2   1 2 3   1 2 3 4

Harmonic Minor

Fingering   2   1 2 3   1 2   3 4

Melodic Minor

Fingering   2 1   2   3   1   2   3 4

Ascending

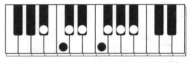

Fingering   2   1 2   3   1 2   3 4

Descending

108

Chord Inversions

B♭ Major

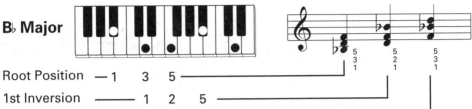

Root Position	— 1	3	5
1st Inversion	1	2	5
2nd Inversion	1	3	5

B♭ Minor

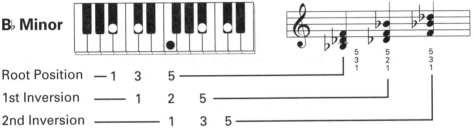

Root Position	— 1	3	5
1st Inversion	1	2	5
2nd Inversion	1	3	5

F Major
(Dominant/V)

E♭ Major
(Subdominant/IV)

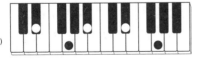

G Minor
(Parallel Minor/VI)

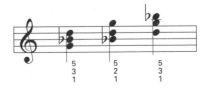

Intervals

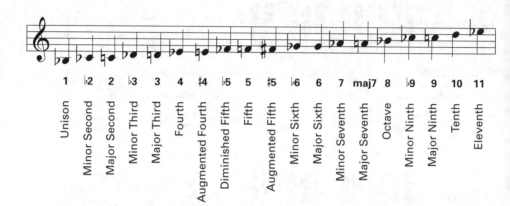

1	♭2	2	♭3	3	4	♯4	♭5	5	♯5	♭6	6	7	maj7	8	♭9	9	10	11
Unison	Minor Second	Major Second	Minor Third	Major Third	Fourth	Augmented Fourth	Diminished Fifth	Fifth	Augmented Fifth	Minor Sixth	Major Sixth	Minor Seventh	Major Seventh	Octave	Minor Ninth	Major Ninth	Tenth	Eleventh

Harmonic Relationships

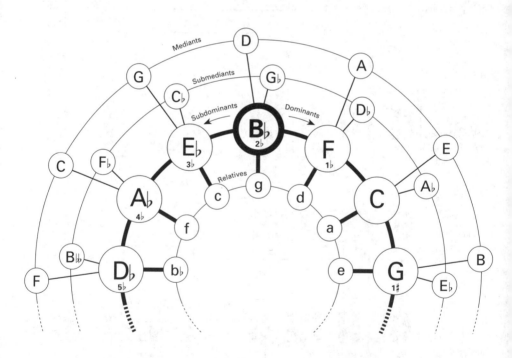

Major Chords

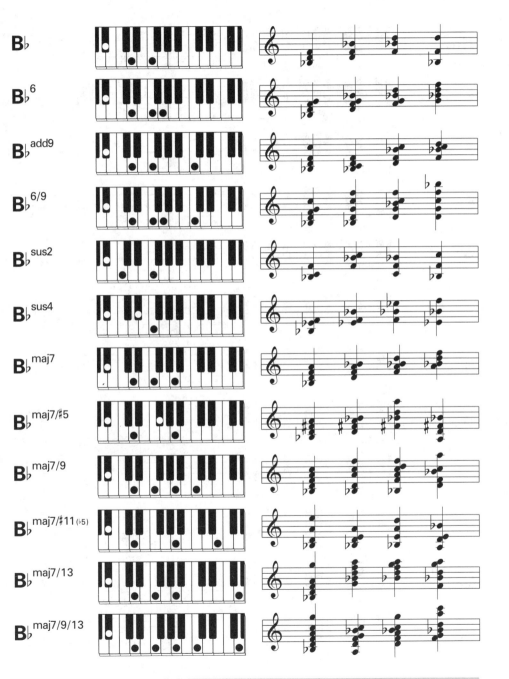

Minor Chords

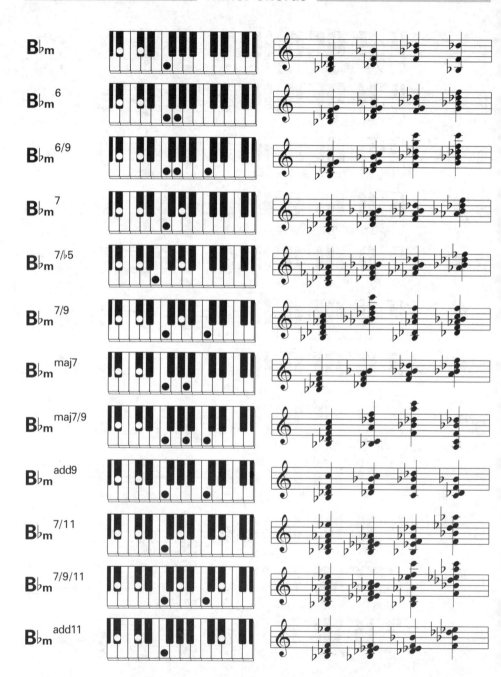

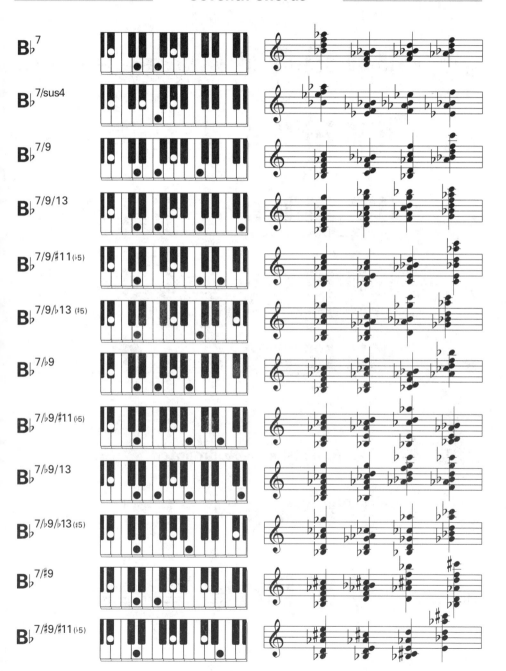

Seventh Chords

Seventh Chords

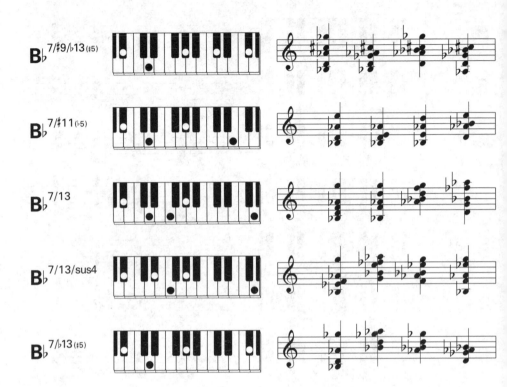

B♭$^{7/♯9/♭13(♯5)}$

B♭$^{7/♯11(♭5)}$

B♭$^{7/13}$

B♭$^{7/13/sus4}$

B♭$^{7/♭13(♯5)}$

Diminished & Augmented

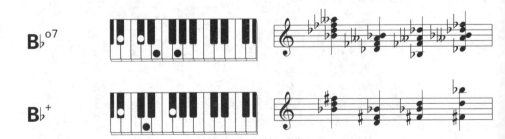

B♭^{o7}

B♭$^{+}$

Scales

Ionian
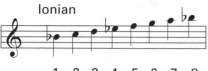

1   2   3   4   5   6   7   8

Dorian

1   2   ♭3   4   5   6   ♭7   8

Phrygian

1   ♭2   ♭3   4   5   ♭6   ♭7   8

Lydian

1   2   3   ♯4   5   6   7   8

Mixolydian

1   2   3   4   5   6   ♭7   8

Aeolian

1   2   ♭3   4   5   ♭6   ♭7   8

Locrian

1   ♭2   ♭3   4   ♭5   ♭6   ♭7   8

HM 3

1   2   3   4   ♯5   6   7   8

HM 5

1   ♭2   3   4   5   ♭6   ♭7   8

MM 7 / Altered

1   ♭2   ♯2   3   ♭5   ♯5   ♭7   8

Major Pentatonic

1   2   3   5   6   8

Minor Pentatonic

1   ♭3   4   5   ♭7   8

Blues Scale

1   ♭3   4   ♭5   5   ♭7   8

Major with Blue Notes

1   2   ↓3   4   ↓5   6   ↓♭7   8

ROOT B

Major Scale

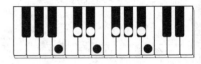

Fingering   1 2 3 1 2 3 4 5

Minor Scales

Natural Minor

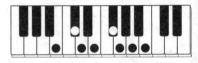

Fingering   1   2 3 1 2 3 4 5

Harmonic Minor

Fingering   1   2 3 1 2 3 4 5

Melodic Minor

Fingering   1 2 3 1 2 3 4 5

Ascending →

Fingering   1 2 3 1 2 3 4 5

← Descending

Chord Inversions

A Major

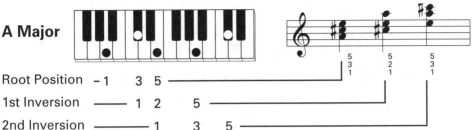

Root Position	– 1	3	5
1st Inversion	1 2		5
2nd Inversion	1	3	5

A Minor

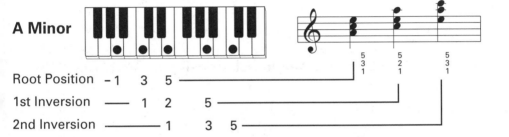

Root Position	– 1	3	5
1st Inversion	1 2		5
2nd Inversion	1	3	5

E Major
(Dominant/V)

D Major
(Subdominant/IV)

F♯ Minor
(Parallel Minor/VI)

Intervals

Harmonic Relationships

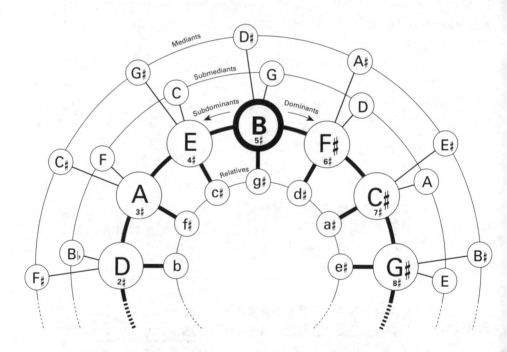

Major Chords

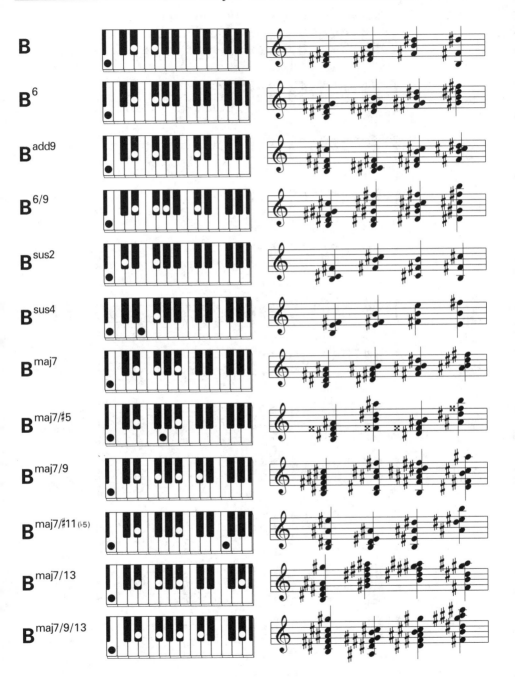

Minor Chords

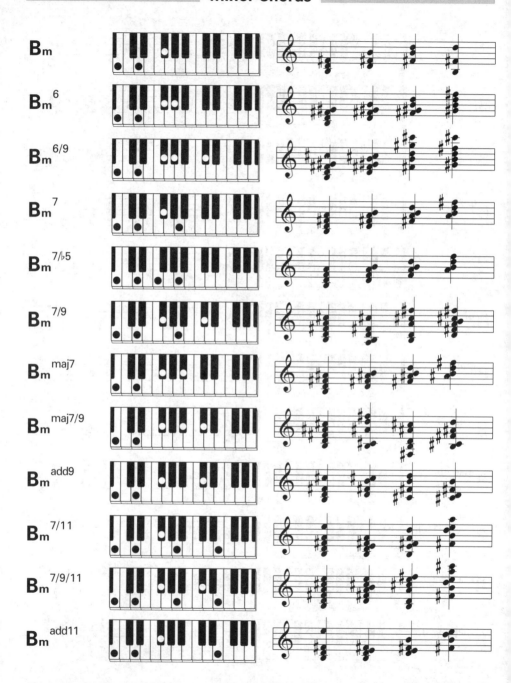

Seventh Chords

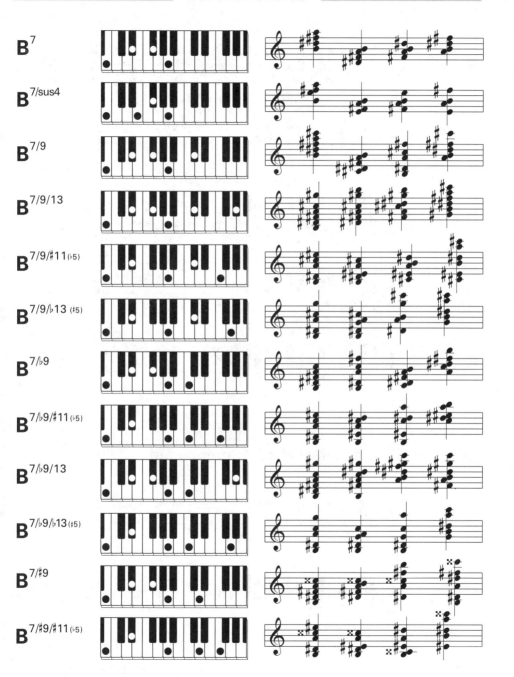

B^7

$B^{7/sus4}$

$B^{7/9}$

$B^{7/9/13}$

$B^{7/9/\#11(\flat 5)}$

$B^{7/9/\flat 13(\#5)}$

$B^{7/\flat 9}$

$B^{7/\flat 9/\#11(\flat 5)}$

$B^{7/\flat 9/13}$

$B^{7/\flat 9/\flat 13(\#5)}$

$B^{7/\#9}$

$B^{7/\#9/\#11(\flat 5)}$

Seventh Chords

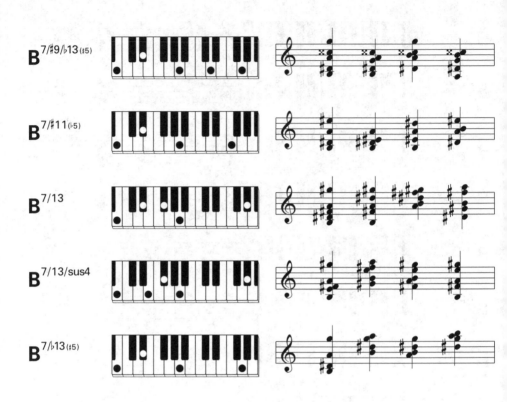

$B^{7/\sharp9/\flat13(\sharp5)}$

$B^{7/\sharp11(\flat5)}$

$B^{7/13}$

$B^{7/13/sus4}$

$B^{7/\flat13(\sharp5)}$

Diminished & Augmented

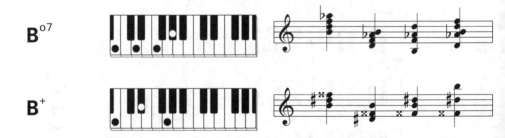

B^{o7}

B^{+}

Scales

Ionian

1 2 3 4 5 6 7 8

Dorian

1 2 ♭3 4 5 6 ♭7 8

Phrygian

1 ♭2 ♭3 4 5 ♭6 ♭7 8

Lydian

1 2 3 ♯4 5 6 7 8

Mixolydian

1 2 3 4 5 6 ♭7 8

Aeolian

1 2 ♭3 4 5 ♭6 ♭7 8

Locrian

1 ♭2 ♭3 4 ♭5 ♭6 ♭7 8

HM 3

1 2 3 4 ♯5 6 7 8

HM 5

1 ♭2 3 4 5 ♭6 ♭7 8

MM 7 / Altered

1 ♭2 ♯2 3 ♭5 ♯5 ♭7 8

Major Pentatonic

1 2 3 5 6 8

Minor Pentatonic

1 ♭3 4 5 ♭7 8

Blues Scale
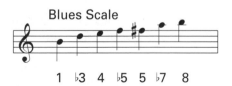

1 ♭3 4 ♭5 5 ♭7 8

Major with Blue Notes

1 2 ↓3 4 ↓5 6 ↓♭7 8

IV. APPENDIX

Chord Synonyms

The dictionary defines synonym (Greek: "bearing the same name") as: identical meaning of two or more different words, for example, "slaughter" and "butcher". In a musical context, this means the following: one and the same chord can have different names, depending on the musician's point of view.

This "point of view" can depend on the harmonic surroundings of the chord, its function in a piece of music or just the musician's fancy (among others).

Here's an example:

The chord C-E-G-A could be called a C6 (a C major chord with an added sixth).

If you wrote down the chord tones of this chord in another order - A-C-E-G - for instance, the same chord would be better called Am7 (an A minor seventh chord).

In this case, C6 and Am7 would be synonyms for one and the same chord, or, to put it in another way, the same chord has two different names.

With a little understanding of chord synonyms, you can greatly expand the possibilities to use the chords you know: the above-mentioned chord could be the tonic chord of a song in the key of C major, the tonic chord of a song in the key of A minor as well as a VI-chord in the key of C major and so forth. This kind of thinking is quite often used in Jazz music and related styles.

Although we can't go into the details in this chord chart, many books are available on the subject, that may help you on your way ...

For a start, you can use the chord synonym chart on the next page to:

  a) find new ways of using chords you already know,
  b) deepen your knowledge about chords and their relationships.

These are just some of the more common chord synonyms to begin with. Once you have mastered the concept of chord synonyms, you'll find it fairly easy to find other ones by yourself.

Chord Synonym Chart (C Major)

Chord Symbol	Chord Tones	Possible Synonyms
sus4	C-F-G	F sus2
6	C-E-G-A	Am 7
6 sus4	C-F-G-A	F add9
6/9 (no root)	E-G-A-D	A 7 sus4
6/9 (no 3)	C-G-A-D	D 7 sus4
6/9 sus4	C-F-A-D	F 6/9
add9 sus4	C-F-G-D	G 7 sus4
minor 6	C-E♭-G-A	Am 7/♭5
minor 7	C-E♭-G-B	E♭ 6
minor 6/9	C-E♭-G-A-D	Am 7/11/♭5
minor 7/13	C-E♭-G-A-B♭	Am 7/♭5/♭9
minor maj7/6	C-E♭-G-A-B	Am 7/9/♭5
minor 7/9 (no root)	(C)-E♭-G-B♭-D	E♭ maj7
minor 7/9/11 (no root)	(C)-E♭-G-B♭-D-F	E♭ maj7/9
7/9/13 (no root)	E-G-B♭-D-A	Gm 6/9
7/♭9 (no root)	(C)-E-G-B♭-D♭	D♭o, Eo, Go, B♭o
7/♭9/♯11 (♭5) (no root)	(C)-E-B♭-D♭-G♭	G♭ 7
7/♯9/♯11 (♭5)	C-E-B♭-D♯-G♭	G♭ 7/6/♯11

Voggenreiter
MADE IN GERMANY

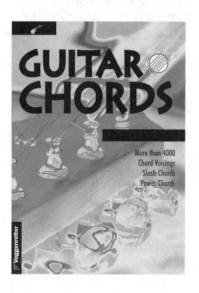

Guitar Chords

This guitar chord reference chart has been especially designed with the working and studying guitarist in mind. It features an overview of more than 4000 chords and their most popular voicings in Rock, Pop and Jazz. Additional chapters on playing techniques, chords synonyms, power chords and slash chords can be helpful to further improve your understanding of music and indiviually enhance your creative potential.

ISBN: 3-8024-0341-X

Easy Rock Bass

This book is a must for the beginning bass player. It not only provides hints on choosing the right instrument, but prepares you for practical exercises and different playing techniques. It also features many examples for practice. The examples are transcribed in standard notation, on tab and on the accompanying cd to which you can either listen or play along to. This book features all the basic techniques of rock, soul, funk, blues and reggae, including: walking bass, double stops and slap/pop.

ISBN: 3-8024-0342-8

Voggenreiter
MADE IN GERMANY

Keyboard Songbook Classic

This songbook contains a selection of some of the most popular classical pieces. It is carefully structured according to the level of difficulty. It can be combined with almost any keyboard method on the market or used as a stand-alone songbook. The notation of each song features standard notation, fingering suggestions, chord diagrams and even information on automation and factory presets. The appendix contains helpful advice on "how to practice", explanations of the most important symbols in tempo and expression notation and an index of the essential terms and chords in "single finger mode", making this book a great learning tool for all keyboarders.

ISBN: 3-8024-0369-X

Solo Solutions 4 Guitar

Solo Solutions is a 3-step guideline for the electric guitar player who intends to develop his solo skills. While the 1st step explains different playing techniques and stylistic devices, the 2nd step is dealing with lead guitar related music theory and scales. The 3rd step combines the two first chapters with countless examples and suggestions on developing your own style. This book features an exclusive hands-on approach, which makes it a great learning tool and a must for the modern guitar player.

ISBN: 3-8024-0344-4

![Voggenreiter — MADE IN GERMANY]

Supersonic Guitar Grooves

The goal of this book is to promote rhythmically and harmonically challenging phrases and licks in order to give you an authentic inside view on seven selected styles.

Live or in a recording session: playing rhythm is the guitarist's main duty. This makes it even harder to understand why most guitarists' rhythm work (frankly) sounds rather unrehearsed and colorless. Especially since working with drum machines and samplers has become a vital part of musical performance, a good sense of rhythm, and some cool licks may just be your "key to success".

ISBN: 3-8024-0343-6

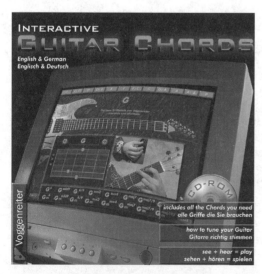

Interactive Guitar Chords - CD-ROM

More than 775 chord voicings are presented in professional quality videos with an easy-to-use interface and "View in View" technique, making practicing a breeze.

A section on music theory contains everything you'll need to know from the absolute beginnings (like tuning your guitar) right up to the creative use of chord voicings.

ISBN: 3-8024-0339-8